Sewing

Techniques and Patterns

Marie-Noëlle Bayard

Photographs by
Charlie Abad

g Co., Inc.
New York

My thanks to Emmanuelle Matas for her effective assistance.

Translated from the French by Ida Amelia Jones and Kelvin K. Wu.

Library of Congress Cataloging-in-Publication Data

Bayard, Marie-Noëlle.
 [Couture. English]
 Sewing : techniques and patterns / Marie-Noëlle Bayard / photographs by Charlie Abad.
   p. cm.
 Includes index.
 ISBN-13: 978-1-4027-3771-8
 ISBN-10: 1-4027-3771-8
 1. Machine sewing.   I. Title.
TT713.B36 2006
646.2—dc22   2006014444

10 9 8 7 6 5 4 3 2 1

Published in 2007 by Sterling Publishing Co., Inc.
387 Park Avenue South, New York, NY 10016
Published originally under the title: *La couture: techniques et modèles*
© 2001 by Place des éditeurs, Paris
English translation copyright: © 2006 by Sterling Publishing Co. Inc.
Distributed in Canada by Sterling Publishing
C/o Canadian Manda Group, 165 Dufferin Street
Toronto, Ontario, Canada M6K 3H6
Distributed in the United Kingdom by GMC Distribution Services,
Castle Place, 166 High Street, Lewes, East Sussex,
England BN7 1XU
Distributed in Australia by Capricorn Link (Australia) Pty. Ltd.
P.O. Box 704, Windsor, NSW 2756, Australia

Printed in China
All rights reserved

Sterling ISBN-13: 978-1-4027-3771-8
     ISBN-10: 1-4027-3771-8

For information about custom editions, special sales, premium and corporate purchases, please contact Sterling Special Sales Department at 800-805-5489 or specialsales@sterlingpub.com

CONTENTS

Introduction

Sewing can be a marvelously creative pastime once the basics have been solidly mastered. It is these basics – along with helpful hints on hand sewing and particularly machine sewing – which I want to impart to my readers. These days, it is hard to imagine sewing without the use of a machine. One of the most indispensable of tools, the sewing machine allows for the rapid, effective completion of the simplest to the most complex projects, even if some stages of preparation or finishing still require your hands-on involvement.

This guide will assist you in improving your expertise. Taking a step-by-step approach, it covers a variety of techniques, offering explanations punctuated with helpful hints and details. Your learning experience is made all the more concrete by the patterns for clothing and home decor that go along with each of these techniques.

The first chapter opens the world of fabrics to you and gives you some pointers on how to distinguish their features. You will also learn to recognize and be instructed in the competent usage of the tools and accessories that comprise and complement the sewing machine.

After reviewing the basics of both hand and machine sewing, you will be able to put your skills into application in later chapters with the benefit of the step-by-step explanations, photos, diagrams, and patterns that accompany the presentation of each new technique. It is by completing the suggested projects, by breaking down the process, and by proceeding step-by-step that you will overcome the aspects of sewing that have been difficult for you. You will also learn that the care and attention that you bring to a task from its inception, far from being trivial, will prove to be most advantageous in the end.

Whether you are in search of an introduction to sewing or a guide to perfecting your skills, this book will pull you into the rich universe of sewing in a technical as well as a creative manner. Once you have solidified your grasp of the basics, you will be able to call upon your imagination, and introduce variations to the patterns to come up with more individualized projects. I am certain that sewing will become more than a pastime for you: It will be one of your true passions, constantly being renewed by the abundance of shapes, materials, textures, and colors in the world.

Marie-Noëlle Bayard

1

SUPPLIES, FABRICS, AND STITCHES

Supplies

PRELIMINARIES

In sewing, no great effort is needed in order to create beautiful results. The secret lies in the right choice of tools and materials and in putting them to good use. Once these basics have been mastered, you can give free reign to your imagination.

So, here is an inventory of the different tools and accessories that will be indispensable in the successful completion of your projects.

MEASURING TOOLS

The **plastic tape measure** is advantageous in that it does not stretch with time and remains accurate so long as you take good care of it. The usual length for a tape measure is 60 inches. If you use a tape with both inches and centimeters, you can work with either metric or inch measurements, noting that in some cases the inches have been rounded off for easier measurements.

Never bend the tape measure; these bends risk marring the surface and making it less legible as time goes on. Be sure to roll it up carefully before putting it away. While working, do as the professional dressmakers do: Place it around your neck; that way, you will always know where it is.

Some tape measures also come in plastic holders or dispensers and will retract into their cases with the simple press of a button.

The **metal measuring stick** should be one yard (or one meter) in length. This trustworthy instrument does not wear down and does not bend. One with a strip of rubber on the underside is preferable. This sole helps prevent the measuring stick from slipping while it is in use.

The **plastic triangle** (isosceles with one right angle) is used to mark and to verify right angles and the straight grain of fabrics. This tool will allow you to mark out 45° angles as well as to cut out strips, bands and other pieces of fabric on the bias with both speed and accuracy.

CUTTING TOOLS

A pair of **dressmaker's scissors** (or tailor's scissors) should have blades that are at least 5 inches in length and ergonomic handles that afford a better grip and a more precise cut. You should pay special care to its purchase.

Choose a model with forged steel blades since they tend to be sturdier than those of cast steel. Use your scissors exclusively for the cutting of fabric; this way, the blades will stay sharp for a longer period of time.

Ordinary scissors are used for cutting through paper, nonwoven items, and other nontextile materials.

Embroidery scissors have tapered, sharply pointed blades. For use in precision work, they are helpful in the opening of buttonholes and in the clipping or notching the rounded seam edges of fabric. Note that some top-of-the-line brands offer models for left-handers.

The **seam ripper** is in the shape of a small fork armed with a sharp edge. Slender and tapered, it allows for the rapid unstitching of machine-sewn straight stitches or satin stitches in a single gesture. You can also use it to open buttonholes.

You may find this accessory in the sewing machine case. If not, this accessory does not cost too much; you should replace it with a new one regularly since the sharp point tends to break and the edge of the blade becomes blunt rather quickly.

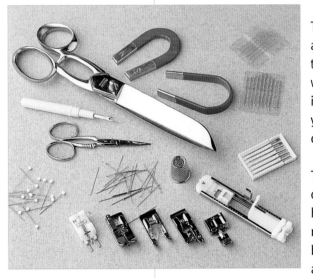

Pinking shears, scissors with blades that produce a zigzag edge, can be used to trim seam allowances after stitching to prevent unraveling, eliminating the need to overcast.

Rotary cutters, used along a metal measuring stick edge, work well to cut long straight edges or make cuts on the bias (as for the Lamp Shade on page 50). For clean cuts, change blades when needed and hold the measuring stick firmly in place, keeping fingers out of the blade's path.

SEWING TOOLS

Steel pins, fine or extra-fine, are used to hold pieces of fabric together before the basting and assembly stages. If you are using a sewing machine for the given project, these pins – on account of their fineness – will allow you to sew all the pieces together directly without having to baste.

Take care to place the pins perpendicular to the edge of the fabric; in this way, the machine needle will not come up against them from above and risk breaking. Throw away bent, rusted, or blunt pins, and do not mix these fine pins with other thicker pins or with those made of brass.

The **pin cushion** with adjustable ring is secured to the wrist of your non-working hand. The cushion allows easy access to your pins and sewing needles.

The **pin magnet,** most often in the form of a horseshoe, is used to recover the contents of a box of pins that has been accidentally overturned.

Assorted needles. Be sure to always keep needles of varying sizes and shapes in your sewing box. Each of the needles is intended for a different purpose:
— Long needles for basting;
— Sewing needles with a finely rubbed-down eye that does not fray the thread. Keep size 7 needles on hand for sewing linen sheets or thick cotton fabrics, size 8 and 9 needles for thinner material, and size 10 needles for delicate fabrics.
Just as you should for pins, throw away bent, blunt, or rusty needles.

The **thimble** often seems unnecessary to beginners; however, it can be of precious assistance. It lets you complete even stitches, baste quickly, and avoid scratching your finger when pushing the eye of the needle through the material.

Choose a metal thimble that is sized to fit around the last joint of your middle finger. Avoid plastic thimbles against which the eye of a needle may slip or slide.

Right-handers should wear the thimble on the third finger of their right hand, and left-handers on the third of their left.

The **needle threader** is a small instrument that consists of a round piece of light metal attached to a thin and flexible piece of metal wire in the shape of a diamond. The wire part of the threader is first pushed through the eye of the needle, after which the thread is slipped through the diamond. When you pull on the round piece, the thread is guided through the eye of the needle.

Tweezers are very effective for pulling out threads cut by a seam ripper when correcting a sewing mistake and can even be used to remove recalcitrant basting threads that still remain after permanent stitching.

The **flat-nosed pliers** allow a covered button to fit together more easily after decorating the shell (the cap or upper portion of the button). See the finishing for the lingerie bag, page 153.

MARKING TOOLS

Light-colored **tailor's chalk** is used on dark fabrics. These days it can come in the form of a pencil, which offers a better grip than the traditional shingle-shaped chalk.

The **drawing pencil** will also be useful for you. A soft lead pencil is perfect for tracing on light-colored fabrics. Also indispensable is the pencil sharpener and sand paper file for sharpening the point of the chalk or the pencil.

The **tracing wheel** complements the dressmaker's carbon paper (see below) for tracing pieces. Select a wheel with teeth that are not too sharp so as not to damage delicate fabrics.

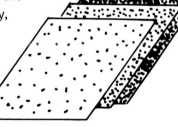

Dressmaker's carbon paper, comes in an envelope containing large sheets in different colors. Light colors are used on dark fabrics and dark colors are used on light materials.

This paper is placed between the pattern and the fabric. After you pass the tracing wheel over the pattern (see right), the tracing paper will leave dots of color on the surface of the textile. Tracing should be done on the back of the fabric; this way, no marks will appear on the front of your work. In any event, the tracings disappear with the first washing.

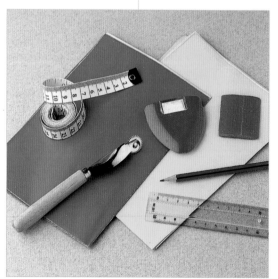

NOTIONS

You can cut **bias binding** from the main fabric or from a coordinate fabric (see the preparation instructions on page 222) for your project, or simply buy some prefolded and ready-to-use bias binding from a notions shop (see the place mats model on page 226).

Tapes and ribbons, whether classic or fancy, exist in a number of materials and colors from which you may make your choice to fit the nature of your project. They are used as finishers or in certain basic techniques such as that of attaching inserts (refer to the explanation on page 216 and the silk stole on page 218).

Piping, braids, tassels, pompons, and other trimming notions are also used for finishing. Choose from an array of possibilities in the notions shop, but also feel free to create your own braid or piping in a fabric of your choice (refer to page 230 for instructions on making piping as well as the curtain tieback, page 232). For the technique for making piped buttonholes, refer to page 178.

Velcro is available in several widths and in a variety of colors. It is made from two adjoining pieces of tape, one of which is covered by ringlet-shaped threads and the other by minuscule hooks; they adhere when they are pressed together.

These bands are self-adhesive, but can also be attached using a straight stitch by hand (or by machine) along the edge. They are used on sports apparel, children's clothes, and some home decor items.

Elastic, cords and strings can be pulled through a hemline to create drawstrings (see the technique on page 236 and the summer pants on page 238).

They also serve to decorate or to reinforce a piece of fabric. Piping is made from a type of cord that you can use to create your own piping (see page 230).

Buttons come in a variety of shapes and sizes. Sew-through, shank, fabric-covered, or novelty, there are buttons to satisfy all tastes (see models page 149 and attachment techniques, page 156).

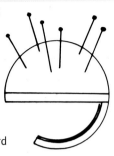

THE MORE YOU KNOW

Put together a complete sewing box, that is, one that contains a specific selection of tools that you may need to use in a wide variety of situations. This box should be handy and remainer within your reach as you work. And be sure to add some standard notions to these basic tools!

Buttons personalize a piece of work and, in part, give it some of its character. See the lingerie bag, page 150, with its buttons being used decoratively, or the child's jacket, page 173, for an example of novelty buttons.

Snap fasteners and hooks and eyes are especially useful for joining two parts of an opening on the side or the edge of a work (see instructions on page 109 or the blouse on page 106).

Zippers, simple or separable, also allow for the joining of the two edges of a fabric in a nonpermanent way.

They are quite practical and can be used with jackets, sports apparel, and home decor items, and various other accessories including bags, slipcovers, bolsters and pillowcases (see instructions on page 162 and the tote bag on page 165).

9

Fabrics

PRELIMINARIES

The choice of fabric varies according to the shape of the garment, the construction techniques that are used and the texture that you desire. You should refer to the instructions that are provided on the pattern envelope or to the specifications for the project for pointers.

If you decide to use a fabric other than what is recommended, choose one that is made from materials that are similar in weight and appearance.

FOR YOUR REFERENCE

Fabric sold by the yard can be bought in specialty shops, in the home decor or notions departments of large retail outlets. If it is decorative textiles that you desire, you might try mail-order catalogs or go online, if you cannot find what you want in boutiques.

Fabric Widths
Fabric widths vary primarily according to their composition: 36 inches and 44 inches are standard widths for cotton, silk, synthetic and other fabrics that are used for fine clothing or everyday wear.

Textiles with 50- to 60-inch and 71-inch widths or wider are generally heavier and are well suited for clothing as well as for home furnishings. Very wide widths, more than 2 yards, are generally reserved for sheeting, batting (for table linens) and synthetic net curtains.

The right side of fabric that has been folded to half-width, and which comes rolled up on a rectangular board, is usually on the inside of the fold that serves as the lengthwise center line. Wool blends, shirt-quality cotton, and some linen mixes, may be folded inward on these bolts of fabric. These pieces are offered in wide widths ranging from 44 inches to 60 inches or more.

Labels
There should be a label attached to one of the two ends of any fabric that you might purchase which indicates the width of the piece, its composition, the percentage breakdown of materials used in its making (in the case of mixed textiles) and the price per yard.

Here are some clarifications on the terms commonly used on labels:
— 100% wool = all wool;
— Pure wool = 95% wool + 5% other materials (these may or may not be listed);
— Wool = 85% wool + 15% other materials;
— Wool blend = between 50% and 84% wool + other materials;

— Wool and acrylic = predominantly wool (and thus quite warm);
— Polyester wool = predominantly polyester (and hence lighter).

The last two usages above are applicable to other blends as well. The dominant material is always listed first on the label. Beginners should give preference to fabrics that do not slip or fray. They should also avoid 100% synthetic fabrics, acetates, fabrics with pile like velvet, as well as knitted fabrics.

FABRIC COMPOSITION

The Four Big Families of Fibers

From the numerous types of fibers in existence, we can distinguish in particular:
— natural animal fibers like silk, wool, cashmere, and vicuna;
— natural plant fibers like cotton, linen, hemp, ramie, and jute;
— artificial chemical fibers that are obtained from cellulose (wood pulp) like viscose, rayon and acetate;
— synthetic fibers that are obtained as the by-products of petroleum processing like polyamide, polyester, acrylic, and polyurethane.

The microfibers that are found in a good number of textures are made up of very light, fine, synthetic fibers, like polar fleece or Lycra.

Fabric Manufacture

We can distinguish among various types of manufacturing:
— woven fabrics that are composed of warp and weft yarns. The threads of these fabric cross in a regular fashion or follow designs of varying complexity, as with the jacquard weave;
— knitted or purled textiles on whose surface the threads form loops. Varying the colors of the threads makes for different designs, as is the case with the jacquard weave. These materials are elastic and of more delicate construction:

— knotted fabrics like lace that are produced by specialized machinery;
— agglomerated (or nonwoven) textiles that incorporate wool or rabbit hair felts, lightweight felts, and certain kinds of interfacing that may be used to line facings.

Textile Treatments

Textiles undergo treatments that give them a number of qualities:
— chemical treatments can make fabrics moth-repellant, stain-resistant, durable, and antiseptic;
— physical treatments can make fabrics waterproof, mat-resistant, pill-resistant, and crease-resistant;
— finishes are treatments that can give new fabrics more decorative or unique features like creasing, crinkling, or moiréing. A rather light finish may be applied to linen or cotton cloth to help these materials maintain their stiffness. Thus, preshrinking a piece of fabric before you attempt to work with it is indispensable (see "Fabric Preparation" on page 12).

LININGS

A good number of articles need to be lined. The reasons are many. Usually it is a matter of hiding the interior construction details found on the wrong side of the fabric and of giving a nice drape to an article. A lining can also give a garment good insulation.

Without exception, the lining must be the same weight as or lighter than the main fabric. It can be cut from fabrics that include a range of fibers: silk (crepe de Chine or pongee) for luxury articles; cotton for sports apparel; wool mixes for winter wear; synthetic fibers (polyamide or polyester) for lighter fabrics.

Make sure that the fiber composition of the lining can withstand the same type of treatment (stain removal, laundering, ironing, etc.) as the main fabric of the article itself. See "Fabric Care" on pages 244–247.

Sewing Garments

The most widely used linings are those made of satin polyester or of polyamide. These plain weave materials, which have a shiny or satiny appearance, are offered in a large array of colors. Pastel or transparent fabrics should be lined with fabrics of an identical or a somewhat lighter color. Dark and opaque fabrics should be lined with fabrics of the same or a contrasting color.

A coat or a winter jacket should be lined with a wool mix, flannel, or with a quilted lining, and, for ease of movement, the sleeves should simply be lined with satin.

Sewing Decorations

Lining is useful in the construction of double curtains. Cotton sateen is most often used for making this item. For curtains that are completely opaque, a "light-absorbent" cloth could be placed between the curtain and the lining.

FABRIC PREPARATION

It is absolutely necessary to prepare the material before proceeding to the cutting and assembly stages. This preparatory phase varies according to the composition of the fibers. Here are some guidelines.

Preshrinking the Fabrics

This process consists of removing the finish that the manufacturer applied to the fabric to stabilize the weave. This can only be done on materials made of natural fibers (wool mixes, cotton blends, linen cloth). Before preshrinking the fabric, test a sample. Cut out a small piece of the fabric measuring 8 inches by 8 inches. Add a few flakes of mild soap to a bath of water and let it soak for 1 hour.

Then remove it from the bath, rinse and lay it out flat to dry. Press it and take its measurements again. If there has been shrinkage, then it will be necessary to preshrink the entire piece of fabric before you work with it.

Before completing your purchase, ask the vendor if the fabric you have chosen has been preshrunk. Most fabrics are preshrunk before they leave the factory. Only linen is not preshrunk in advance because that runs the risk of it's creasing before it is even sold. To preshrink linen, submerge it overnight in clear water with soap flakes. The piece must be soaked flat. For large lengths of cloth, use the bathtub. Rinse and spread the piece out, but make sure to keep it flat; avoid wringing so as not to mark the cloth. Press while still slightly damp.

Textiles that need to be dry-cleaned, like silk, must be dampened. Blot them using a damp piece of cloth. Dry flat and iron on the wrong side.

Rectifying Edges

It is absolutely necessary to ensure that the edges of a piece of fabric are perfectly straight. Press to remove all traces of folding before you cut. Adjust the edges so they are aligned on the straight grain. Cut across the fabric about 4 inches in from one end. With the aid of a pin, loosen and then pull up a weft (cross) thread; removing it entirely. Cut the fabric by following the track left by the thread that you removed. Square sides by trimming off the selvage and pulling a warp (lengthwise) thread in the same manner.

For fabrics with a locked weft, there is another method that can be used. Notch the fabric about 4 inches in from the edge then, holding one edge of the notch in each hand, tear the cloth. For fabrics printed with regular designs, cut the edges along a row of the design; this will serve as a guide.

CUTTING THE FABRIC

Transferring the Pattern Outlines

Pin the enlarged pattern pieces to the fabric and trace their outlines with tailor's chalk. With dressmaker's carbon paper, mark all the guidelines, such as darts, hemlines, and facing lines.

Cutting the Pieces

Once the marking is complete, cut the pieces out with the dressmaker's scissors:
— If the pattern does not explicitly include lines for seam allowances, cut the pieces of fabric ⅝ inch beyond the trace marks.
— If these allowances are specified, the pieces of the pattern should be bordered by a double line.

The inner line corresponds to the seam line; the outer line is the cutting line. Mark these two parallel lines with the chalk and cut along the outer line. With the fabric laid out flat on the table, slide the blade of the scissors under the fabric and cut. In order to obtain precise results, leave this blade in contact with the table.

Do **not** forget to make allowances for layers of interfacing or interlining if they are needed to complete your project. These pieces allow for a better fit and/or finishing of more delicate parts like collars, cuffs, and hemlines.

OVERCASTING

Overcasting consists of stitching around the border of each piece, in order to avoid the fabric's becoming frayed. This stage often takes place before an article is actually put together. Overcasting can be done either by hand or by machine.

Overcasting by hand is necessary in any case where overcasting by machine would be impossible. For best results, overcast the fabric in the direction of the ravels. The stitch is done along the length of the edge from left to right and overlaps one layer when the piece has just been cut, or two layers after assembly.

First make a vertical stitch, then complete a second stitch about ¼ inch from the first while pulling the length of thread to the right. The thread should cause a slanted stitch to appear. Smoothly pull the needle through so as to leave the edge of the fabric flat.

Overcasting by machine is done on the zigzag setting. Adjust the machine according to the thickness of the fabric: wide overcasting for thick fabrics and narrow overcasting for thinner fabrics. Keep the edge of the fabric centered under the presser foot and stitch. You should not let the edge of the fabric pull up. If it does, adjust the stitch by increasing or reducing its width and length.

THE MORE YOU KNOW

If you are in doubt as to the exact amount of fabric that you need to get, ask the vendor if the fabric you have chosen is usually in stock. If there is no guarantee that it will be restocked, buy ½ to 1 yard more fabric than is needed upfront. In addition, always choose your fabric by the light of day. Very often, the artificial lighting in department stores modifies the colors, and you run the risk of returning home, only to find yourself with a fabric that does not exactly correspond to what you wanted.

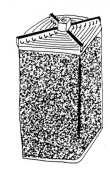

The overedge elastic stitch is used mainly with fabrics cut on the bias. These are overcast by machine with the elastic stitch (see page 26) in order to prevent the edges of the fabric from stretching. If your sewing machine does not possess this function, do a loose overcasting by hand.

Invisible Mending by Flame
Certain synthetic fabrics do not need to be overcast; passing the flame of a match along their edge is sufficient for mending. It is recommended that you first try this on a sample to determine how the material will react to the flame.

13

The Pattern

PRELIMINARIES

You will find patterns for clothing and for decorations in notions shops, or boutiques that sell fabric by the meter (or the yard). You can consult the retailers' catalog for the pattern brands that they carry, right there in the store.

Most stores publish one or two catalogs per year, sometimes one per season. Some of them even offer brochures individually dedicated to home furnishings or ready-made clothing for women, children and men.

CHOOSING A PATTERN

The Pattern Size

The size of the model should be clearly marked on the envelope, and a table of measurements should accompany the pattern. Make sure that these measurements correspond to those you would like to have (see measurements, page 247). Standardization has reduced the differences in sizing across stores, but a few inconsistencies still persist and some brands may suit you better than others.

If you are debating between two sizes, go with the larger of the two. It is always easier to make alterations by reducing rather than by enlarging pattern pieces. If the measurements of the top and bottom portions of your body differ, buy a pattern in each size, for example, a 12 for the top and a 14 for the bottom. This is more costly, but the results will be worth it.

Another possibility to consider is a multisized pattern, on which each size is represented by a different line (solid, dotted…) or by a different color.

The Pattern Description

You should find a diagram indicating the main seams of the pattern on the description that comes with it. If seams are included in the diagram, you should see a single line that corresponds to the cutting line; seam allowances and hemlines will be indicated separately. On good-quality patterns, the contours of the pieces are bordered with two lines. On a pattern piece, the inner line is the seam line, the outer line is the cutting line.

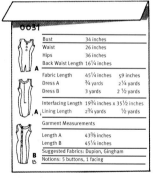

Bust	34 inches	
Waist	26 inches	
Hips	36 inches	
Back Waist Length	16¼ inches	
Fabric Length	45¼ inches	59 inches
Dress A	¾ yards	2¼ yards
Dress B	3 yards	2½ yards
Interfacing Length	19¾ inches x 35½ inches	
Lining Length	2¾ yards	½ yards
Garment Measurements		
Length A	43⅜ inches	
Length B	45¼ inches	
Suggested Fabrics: Dupion, Gingham		
Notions: 5 buttons, 1 facing		

The instructions should also clearly indicate the fabric choices that are compatible with the model, as well as a step-by-step guide to how the pieces are to be joined. Finally, the pattern should come with a cutting plan that provides instructions specific to the type of fabric that is to be used (plain, printed, with or without nap) and its width: 36 inches; 44–45 inches; 54 inches; 50–60 inches, etc.

TRANSFERRING THE PATTERN

Tracing onto Tissue Paper

Some patterns need to be traced onto a sheet of tissue paper. Pattern pieces, which often overlap and are sometimes even superimposed, can be distinguished by their individual markers: hatched lines, dashed lines, dotted lines, as well as numbers or letters.

Get yourself some large sheets of tissue paper from the notions shop. Before transferring the pattern pieces, press the paper with a dry iron on the "silk" setting. Lay the sheet of paper on a table, securing it on two sides with pieces of adhesive tape, and slide the pattern underneath. Transfer the outlines of the pattern pieces onto the paper using a drawing pencil. Indicate the assembly markers, the names of the pattern pieces, their letter or number, the straight grain, and finally the dart or fold lines. Use a ruler to help you with the straight lines. Transfer each piece separately, and cut it out along the outer edge of the trace line.

Modifying a Pattern Piece

The method for transferring the pattern that is presented here can also be used with traditional patterns where a piece needs to be modified—for example, enlarged or reduced. Transfer the outline of the pattern pieces onto a sheet of tissue paper with a drawing pencil, then make the necessary adjustments. When you have finished, erase the initial trace lines in the areas that have been adjusted before cutting along the outer edges of the piece. With a multisized pattern, cut the pieces out along the line corresponding to your size, differentiating if necessary between the sizing lines for the top and the bottom parts of your body.

POSITIONING THE PATTERN PIECES

If your pattern does not contain a cutting layout indicating the width of the fabric between the selvages and the direction of the fabric, here are some specifics:
— fold the fabric in two, lengthwise, right side in;

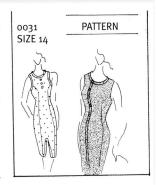

THE MORE YOU KNOW
The photograph or the drawing that accompanies the pattern specifies certain details of cutting and assembly, such as the shape of the collar, button tabs, sleeves, pockets, etc. Pay attention to all these details, because it is these details that differentiate this pattern from another one. Beginners should give preference to simple forms as single-breasted jackets, patch pockets, straight skirts, and gathered dresses.

— first select the pieces of the pattern containing a "center" line (often a dotted line along an outer edge); place them over the fabric fold line. The other pieces should be arranged around these;
— position each pattern piece according to the straight grain indicator that is on it; the indicator should stay perfectly parallel to the straight grain of the fabric.

The rules outlined below are to be followed according to the kind of work aids you have:
— For napped or directional fabrics (velvet, satin, prints, gabardine, imitation fur or faux-fur, etc.) make sure that all the pattern pieces are placed in the right direction before cutting. Anticipate a little more length for these than for other fabrics so you have room to cut out each piece in the correct direction;
— On fabrics that have symmetric lines, the pattern pieces can be placed head to tail;
— When you fold checkered fabrics in two, ensure that the horizontal and vertical lines coincide on the width as well as on the length;
— On printed fabrics that have direction, arrange all the pieces in the same direction.

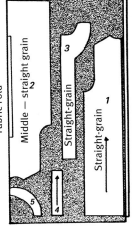

Interfacing

PRELIMINARIES

Interfacing involves the fitting of a piece of stiff material in between two layers of fabric to give body, shape and support to an item after sewing.

Nonwoven interfacing comes in a variety of weights and two colors – black or white – and may be used to interface all sorts of materials. The fusible types are highly practical and are usually intended for use in collars or cuffs where they are preferable to facings, which tend to crinkle with use.

CHOOSING AND CUTTING THE INTERFACING

Choosing the Interfacing

Several kinds of materials can be used depending on the nature and the thickness of the fabric that is to be interfaced:
— Thick wool blends are interfaced with thick cotton cloth, linen cloth, hair canvas, or with thick nonwoven materials especially suited to wool blends;
— Wool blends of average thickness and cotton fabrics are interfaced with the aid of permanently starched cotton or with thin nonwoven stiffening;
— Silks and light fabrics are interfaced with organdy, batiste (for cotton cloths) or organza (for silks).

Cutting the Interfacing

Interfacing has to be inserted between the internal contours of the piece to be assembled. Cut it to within ⅛ inch of the exact edges of the piece being interfaced in order to avoid catching it in the seams.

Cutting can be done on the grain or on the bias, according to the nature of the piece to be interfaced:
— Cut the interfacing following the straight grain marking on the pattern for the main pieces.
— Cut the interfacing on the bias to line collars, sleeve ends, jacket lapels, and hemlines.

APPLYING INTERFACING

Attaching Sew-on Interfacing

After cutting the interfacing, lay it out on the back of the fabric. Keep it in place using a few pins, and attach the edges of the interfacing to the

main fabric with a herringbone stitch (see the description on page 23).

The first part of the stitch is stitched into the fabric, while the second part of the stitch only goes through the interfacing. Make small stitches in the fabric that are in line with the stitching of the seam line. After assembly, the stitches that make up the seam should be completely invisible.

Applying Fusible Interfacing

Cut the piece of interfacing along the tracings that appear on its wrong side. Adjust the iron to a temperature setting that is suitable for the composition of the main fabric. Lay the adhesive side of the interfacing against the wrong side of the fabric and pass the iron over it for a period of about 10 seconds. Lifting the iron with each move, work the iron little by little over the surface to be interfaced; do not slide the iron. Each placement of the plate of the iron on the interfacing should overlap the preceding one (see the diagram below).

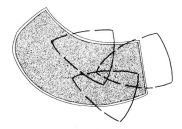

When the interfacing has been completely applied, wait half an hour before continuing with assembly to permit the resins in the adhesive of the interfacing to cool completely.

JOINING TWO PIECES OF INTERFACING

It is sometimes necessary to connect two pieces of interfacing. Here are two different ways in which this can be done.

The Lapped Seam Technique

Lay the edge of the first piece over the edge of the second such to create an overlap of ¼ inch. Secure the pieces in place with either a zigzag stitch by machine or a herringbone stitch by hand.

THE MORE YOU KNOW

In order to stabilize the interfacing and to prevent it from slipping against the fabric, keep the edges in place using a herringbone stitch. Certain types of interfacing, called fusibles, are applied with an iron. Fusibles let you skip over the hand sewing steps, but are not suitable for fine fabrics and fabrics that contain silk because the adhesive contained in the interfacing may leave a mark on them.

The Abutted Seam Technique

Align the edges of the two pieces. Lay a ⅜-inch wide strip of bias-cut fabric over this boundary. Baste the strip of bias, stitching along both of its edges, then complete a zigzag stitch to join the two pieces of interfacing.

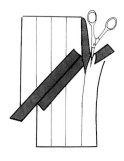

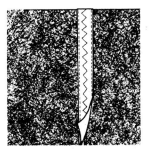

Note that a fusible interfacing is always applied to the wrong side of the fabric; also the edges are joined with the layers face-to-face to each other.

The Sewing Machine

PRELIMINARIES

The components found on a sewing machine can vary depending upon its brand, but even the most basic of machines will feature a given set of them. They are described below.

Note that on electronic machines, adjustments (to the stitch width, etc.) are made from a digitized control panel.

DESCRIPTION OF THE SEWING MACHINE

The **power cord** is made up of two leads that are connected to a central plug. One of the leads carries a plug that connects into the power supply. The other lead connects the machine to the pedal.

The **plate** situated under the presser foot has grooved, graduated guiding lines which let you make seams of different widths. By using these marks, you can obtain perfectly straight stitches. The first part of the plate is fixed in place; it has two slotted openings that allow the teeth of the feed to pass through and an opening for the needle so that the needle can pick up the bobbin thread. The second part of the plate slides outward to yield access to the bobbin spool.

The **flat bed** on which your work is placed can be reduced to a free arm, which facilitates the stitching of certain curved or rounded parts like cuffs or the bottoms of pants.

The **needle arm** carries a clamp which, when loosened, allows the needle to be removed from its casing.

The **presser foot** is equipped with a lever so that it can be raised and lowered for precise positioning over the fabric.

The **tension regulator** of the bobbin thread is calibrated. Certain stitches, as well as the working of certain textiles, require a specific tension setting. If the bobbin thread can be seen on the top side of the stitching, it means that you need to increase the tension in the thread.

The **needle lever** should always be in its up position when you want to remove your work from the machine; the lever lifts the needle and frees the fabric.

The **bobbin filling system and thread guide** allow for the smooth and rapid filling of the bobbin with machine-type thread.

The **bobbin thread guide** regulates the tension in the thread, which is indispensable for achieving an even stitch (see thread tensions, page 82).

The touch screen allows for stitch or embroidery selection and for adjusting the settings of a stitch.

The **operating keys** located near the needle and the presser-foot allow for easy access to the thread-cutting, backstitching and needle-raising functions of the machine.

The **bobbin pins** are mounted horizontally or vertically on the sewing machine depending upon the model. These pins serve two purposes: the first is to maintain the thread of the bobbin in its place; the second is to allow for the automatic refilling of bobbin spools.

The balance or hand wheel, also called the **fly-wheel,** serves to feed thread and/or fabric through the machine. On older sewing machine models, it can be controlled by hand and adjusted either at the beginning or at the end of a work session.

The **speed control lever** controls the selection of the sewing speed. There are three settings: slow, standard (or medium) and fast.

The **thread cutter** is situated in close proximity to the needle and allows for the quick and easy cutting of thread (see above, "Operating Keys").

The **main switch** allows for the turning on and off of the sewing machine at any given time.

The **feed button** serves to turn on/off the feed on the sewing machine as necessary.

A CLOSE-UP OF SOME COMPONENTS

The Machine Spool

This part is either made of transparent plastic or metal. Depending upon the thickness of the thread used, a full spool contains from 27 to 65 yards of thread. To refill the spool, place the bobbin and the spool of thread on their respective pins. Pass the thread through the thread guide. Wrap a small amount of thread around the center of the bobbin spool. Make a few turns and then secure the end of the thread in the slot situated under the spool pin.

Filling the Machine Spool

Push the pin with the machine spool into its corresponding slot. The screen will then show a drawing of the spool. Push lightly on the pedal and verify that the bobbin is being evenly filled. The thread winds up forming layers that should completely cover the height of the spool.

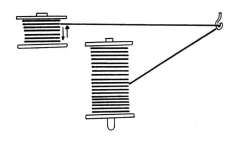

The Bobbin Case

Once the bobbin has been filled, the bobbin stops automatically. Cut the thread and remove the bobbin from its pin. Place the bobbin in its case, under the guide plate, paying attention to the direction in which the bobbin thread will unwind. You should take care to keep this case free of lint.

THE MORE YOU KNOW

Before beginning a task, set the sewing machine up with the thread that is best suited to your project. To thread the machine, complete these steps in the order indicated. Pass the bobbin thread through all of the thread guides, referring as necessary to the manual that came with your sewing machine. This process can vary from one model to the next.

The Feed or Feed Dogs or Feed Teeth
The feed dogs are made of pieces of steel and come with fine, sharp teeth. Their characteristic to-and-fro movement guides the fabric under the presser foot. The action of the feed dogs can be turned off, in which case your work would then be guided through entirely by hand.

Adjusting the Stitch and the Presser Foot
The feed dogs are associated with the regulation of the stitch width and length as well as with the pressure of the presser foot. For example, when you complete a backstitch, it is the feed dogs that reverse the direction in which the fabric moves under the presser foot.

To mend an item or to complete some kinds of "free" embroidery stitches, you must turn off the feed and guide the fabric through with your hands. The feed dogs can be turned off using a lever provided especially for this purpose.

Care and Maintenance of the Feed Dogs
In order to keep the feed dogs at their sharpest, avoid direct contact between the dogs and metallic items like the sole of the presser foot. Place a piece of fabric between the sole and the feed dogs when the machine is not in use. Avoid empty stitching at the end of a stitch and stitching over pins that are too thick. In any event, it is possible to change the feed dogs whenever they become blunt.

MACHINE NEEDLES

Choosing the Needle
Be sure to install a suitable needle. Choose a needle based upon the thickness of the fabric and the thread. You should change dull or bent needles since they run the risk of damaging the fabric or causing skipped stitches.

On most of the newer sewing machines, threading is done from front to back. On older models, threading is done from right to left.

Needle Numbering
Nowadays, needle numbering has been standardized. In the store you can find sewing machine needles under the following reference listings:
— Extra-fine size 60 needles for light fabrics
— Size 70 and size 80 needles for cotton fabrics
— Size 90 and size 100 needles for draperies
— Size 110 and size 120 needles for sewing through thick layers, as might be needed to complete the seams on a pair of jeans.

Kinds of Needles
Specialized needles are available for some materials: the bevel-edged point for synthetic fabrics, the ball point for knitted fabrics, the helical point for leathers, the saber point for the piercing of openwork, etc. A few sewing machines permit the use of double needles for double stitching work.

THE PRESSER FOOT OR SEWING FOOT

The Presser Foot of the Sewing Machine
The foot is held in place by a clamp or a lever on the presser foot bar; or it may just simply snap into place. You can select from a variety of presser feet depending upon the fabric, the finishing, or the stitches you would like to use. You can also make use of the edges of the presser foot to help you stitch in a straight line; you should keep a close eye on the presser foot rather than the needle as you stitch. You can also use the graduated guiding lines of the plate to help you.

Choosing the Presser Foot

You will find several presser feet in the box of accessories that came with your machine. Here is a list of the principal ones; the manufacturer may also offer other kinds of feet for specific purposes. Any presser foot can be bought separately.

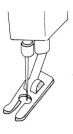

The **general purpose foot,** which comes in metal or transparent plastic, has an oval hole that allows you to execute classic stitches like the zigzag stitch as the needle is put in a position to travel a lateral path through the fabric.

The **zipper foot**, which is thin and narrow, is especially designed for applying both piping and zippers.

The special purpose foot or **satin stitch foot,** made of transparent plastic, features a grooved sole which makes it possible for the embossment of the satin stitch to pass through underneath. It can also handle some extra-thick fabrics.

The **buttonhole foot** is large and has a sole that is characterized by two underlying hollows that prevent the stitch from being flattened as you work.

A **nonstick foot** (like the Teflon-soled foot, for example) eases the assembly of glazed or plastic-coated fabrics.

The darning or **embroidery foot,** which can be either round or square, is completely empty in the middle. While it is used for free embroidery, it can also be used for mending.

The **roller foot** simultaneously guides two fabrics or a main fabric and its lining through the sewing machine.

The **quilting foo**t makes it possible to obtain beautiful quilting and fleece interlining work. It can also produce a nice topstitch on thick fabrics.

Hand Stitches

PRELIMINARIES

Even if you sew your work on the machine, certain stages of assembly or finishing are best completed by hand.

Presented below are the basic stitches with which you should absolutely familiarize yourself. For each stitch, an indication of its most common uses and guidelines for completing it are given, in addition to a diagram.

THE STRAIGHT STITCH OR RUNNING STITCH

This stitch is used for:
— Tacking or basting: Stitches are about ¼ inch in length; they do not need to be even, since they will eventually be removed;
— Seams (for small-sized jobs): Even stitches ¹⁄₁₆ to ⅛ inch in length
— Gathers: Even stitches ¹⁄₁₆ inch in length;
— Mending: Stitches ¹⁄₁₆ inch in length; each separated by ¼ inch; the stitches of the rows abut on each other and alternate.

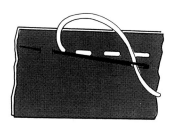

Using a Running Stitch for Basting
Work from right to left. The two pieces of fabric are held together with pins. Make large running stitches. Every 4 inches, pull the needle smoothly through the fabric. Use a long, fine needle.

Using a Running Stitch for Sewing a Seam
The stitch is worked from right to left. In order to execute an even stitch, keep the two superimposed layers of fabric in the left hand, between the thumb and the index finger. Make small stitches, pushing the needle through with the thimble. To make an even stitch, insert the needle perpendicularly into the fabric. Bring the needle out on the trace line, and reinsert it at a point about ¹⁄₁₆ inch farther along. The needle will reappear on the right side of the fabric, sliding along the nail of the left thumb (if you are right-handed). Work two or three stitches at a time, then pull the needle smoothly through to keep the fabric from puckering.

THE BACKSTITCH

The backstitch is used for certain aspects of sewing. Make very even stitches, of about ⅛ inch in length. This stitch, which imitates the machine running stitch, is used for making strong seams or for attaching zippers.

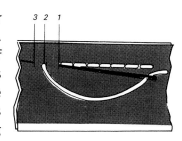

Execution

Work from right to left. Bring the needle through on the seam line at position 2 (see diagram). Insert the needle perpendicularly into the two fabrics to be assembled, about ⅛ inch from the right edge, and behind to the right of the previous entry point (position 1). Bring the needle through again toward the left, and about ⅛ inch ahead of the first stitch (position 3). Pull the needle through and reinsert it in the same hole as the first stitch (position 2). Continue in this manner until the seam is completed. Use a thimble to help you to push the eye of the needle through the fabric.

THE HEMMING STITCH OR SLIPSTITCH

This stitch is used for:
— Ordinary hems;
— The hems of linings;
— Turning a piece of bias inside out.

Execution

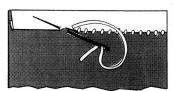

Work from right to left, with the hem pointing up. Push your needle in to the right, under the hem, and bring it through again a few millimeters (or eighths of an inch) to the left. Stitch into the thickness of the garment or along the edge of the fold of the lining. Use the thimble to push the eye of the needle through, picking up a little of the thickness of the hem in the process. The stitches along the inside of the hem should be long and on the bias, while those that are visible should be small and straight.

THE HERRINGBONE STITCH OR BLIND HEM STITCH

This stitch is used for:
— Keeping two layers of fabric flat without folding the edges together;
— Making a hem that will then be covered by a lining;
— Mounting grosgrain on a belt or a waistband.

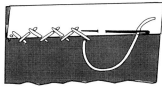

The needle you choose should be suited to the type of fabric with which you are working (natural fibers, synthetics, technical, coated etc.) and to the nature of the work you are doing (basting; plain, double or triple seams; embroidery; topstitching; buttonholing; button attachment, etc.). For guidelines on choosing thread, refer to the thread lexicon on page 251; for guidelines on choosing needles, see "Sewing Tools" on page 7.

Execution

The herringbone stitch is worked from left to right, along two parallel lines. Smoothly pull the needle through, so as not to cause the material to pucker. Begin with a backstitch hidden in the thickness of the hem, on the left edge.

The first part of the stitch is made on the lower line; the second line is situated about ¼ inch above the first line. On the lower line, make a tiny horizontal backstitch. Make another small backstitch on the upper line through only the hem layer and to the right of the previous stitch on the lower line. Repeat, keeping stitches evenly spaced. Large, slanted, crossed stitches will be formed on the wrong side of the piece, while one line of tiny straight stitches will be created on the right side of the work.

THE BLANKET STITCH

This stitch is used for:
— Loops used in place of buttonholes;
— Loops used as the eye part of hooks and eyes for fastening a tab.

Execution

The blanket stitch is worked from left to right. Begin with two or three large stitches the width of the desired loop, and keep these in place with a

few backstitches made in the fabric.

Insert the needle vertically into the fabric. Bring it out to the left (at position 1 in the diagram), reinsert the needle vertically behind the thread loops (positions 2 and 3) and slip the thread under the point of the needle. With the left thumb, keep the loop in place while smoothly pulling the thread through. Align the stitches against each other to cover the entire surface of the loop.

THE BUTTONHOLE STITCH

Most sewing machines are limited to making ordinary buttonholes. When confectioning elegant attire or lingerie, it is sometimes preferable to make the buttonholes by hand.

Prepare the buttonhole by passing a basting thread over the tracing line of the slot. Mark off the length of the buttonhole with a perpendicular stitch at each end of the basting. Cut the buttonhole with narrow scissors. Turn down the edges with an iron, then outline the edge of the buttonhole with a straight stitch.

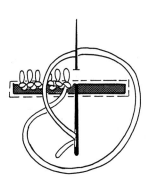

Execution

The buttonhole stitch is worked from left to right, beginning with the top part of the edge. Bring the needle out under the opening, on the left edge. Insert the needle vertically from the top down (not as shown in the diagram), and slide the thread under the point of the needle. Smoothly pull the needle through in the direction of the opening so that the loop comes to rest on the edge of the buttonhole. With the left thumb, keep the loop against the surface of the fabric, while pulling the thread.

Put the stitches close against each other and make them all of the same height.

When you reach the corner of the buttonhole, fan the stitches out around the edge. At the other end of the buttonhole, make two backstitches and form small stitches perpendicular to those lining the opening. Turn work to stitch the opposite edge. Knots should be directed toward the edge of the opening.

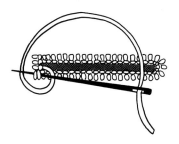

UNDERLINING AND LINING

These terms are often confused; however, each has its own definition:

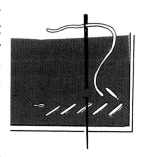

Underlining consists of keeping a fabric and its lining together during the assembly stage. This operation is indispensable, especially for articles with curved outlines, and makes for a lining that matches its piece of fabric exactly. Make large, oblique basting stitches, being sure to stitch through both layers. When the work is complete, remove the basting.

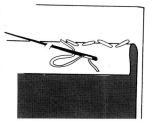

Lining consists of joining two fabrics by working on the wrong side of the fabrics. For example, you might use a slipstitch for a hem and a basting stitch to keep a fleece interlining in place on a double curtain. This assembly, unlike the preceding one, remains in place once the work has been completed.

Machine Stitches

PRELIMINARIES

Machine stitches have things in common with hand stitches bearing the same name, but sometimes they present a few differences apart from the equipment used. And so, the decision: Hand sew, or machine stitch?

Ultimately, the choice is up to you, based on the project, the phase of production that the piece is in, and your preferences.

THE STRAIGHT STITCH OR RUNNING STITCH

This is the basic stitch. It should be perfectly flat, and should not cause the fabric to gather or pucker up (see adjusting the thread tension on page 82). Begin and end the stitch with a few stitches made by going backward. Cut the thread close to the seam. The straight stitch can also be used for basting and for gathering.

To baste, adjust the stitch to its longest and slightly loosen the tension of the top thread. Do not make a backstitch at the beginning and the end of the seam, so that you will be able to remove the thread easily.

For making gathers, follow the same procedure as above, except that you will make a backstitch at the beginning of the stitch. Stitch, then pull the spool thread in order to gather the fabric. It is advisable to put a thicker thread on the spool than in the bobbin.

THE ZIGZAG STITCH

This stitch has a variety of uses. Both its length and width can be regulated according to the effect desired. In order to work this stitch, install the standard presser foot or the special purpose foot, and make a few backstitches in order to knot off the threads at the end of the stitch.

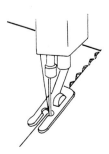

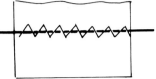

In order to make gathers, the most commonly used stitch is the straight stitch (also called the running stitch). However, there is another method, which consists of sliding a piece of fine pearlized cotton thread through a zigzag stitch. Make sure that you do not directly stitch through the pearlized thread. Pull to form the gathers. This method lends a certain suppleness to the piece and is particularly suitable for delicate textiles.

THE ELASTIC STITCH

This method of stitching allows for the assembly of tricots or knitted fabrics. Adjust the machine to a narrow zigzag stitch (stitch length, 1/16 inch; width, 1/32 to 1/16 inch), to get a supple seam. This adjustment applies to fabrics assembled on the bias.

THE BLIND HEMSTITCH OR ZIGZAG BLIND HEMSTITCH

This stitch is found on numerous machines. It is made up of four straight stitches and a zigzag stitch, or four small zigzag stitches and a fifth, larger one. Install a presser foot for making "blind hems." Load the spool with nylon thread. Adjust the width of the stitch to a width of your choice, between 1/32 and 1/8 inch. This stitch is worked by placing the presser foot so that it straddles the edge of the fold for the hemline.

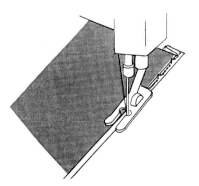

THE SATIN STITCH

This stitch offers a beautiful finish. Install the satin stitch foot; adjust the length of the stitch to almost zero ("o") and the width of the stitch according to the desired effect. Do not pull on or push the fabric; allow the feed to do its job. Keep the material in place by placing your hands flat on either side of the presser foot. The stitch will advance slowly, but do not let the stitches be made on top of each other. Set the speed to the maximum.

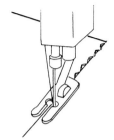

If the fabric is thin, there is the risk that it will shirr. To avoid this, place a thin piece of artist's tracing paper (or tissue paper) between the fabric and the presser foot. When work is completed, tear away the paper to remove it.

BUTTONHOLING

These can be made on the machine, by adjusting the satin stitch so that it is not so tightly locked, in this way imitating hand buttonholing. Prepare the buttonhole with a basting done by hand, to determine the length of the buttonhole. Next, embroider, using the machine satin stitch, and then open the buttonhole using a cutter or a seam ripper.

Insert the point of the tool at one end of the buttonhole and push gently. When you arrive at the center of the buttonhole, remove the tool and start again from the other end of the buttonhole. Do not cut the threads which have just been embroidered.

2

ASSEMBLY WITH BASIC SEAMS

The Double Topstitched Seam

PRELIMINARIES

The double topstitched seam shows up on the top of your finished work. In addition to being decorative, it helps flatten out the thickness of an assembly.

Here are two good pieces of basic advice:

– Use a simple synthetic, twisted, or corded thread, according to the nature of the fabric. Choose one in a color that matches or contrasts against the base color.

– To reinforce the decorative side of the double topstitched seam on a cotton fabric, place a thick string in the bobbin and fill the spool with a simple thread. Use a needle with a large eye (size 100 or 120) to prevent fraying of the thick thread during your work.

MORE ABOUT THE TECHNIQUE

The double topstitched seam is made in three steps. The first step consists of a simple assembly. Once the seam has been pressed open, a second stitching using a fancy thread is made on each side, through the allowances of the previous seam. These are the second and third steps.

STEP 1

Place the fabrics edge to edge, with the right sides facing each other. Pin together, or baste.

Stitch ⅝ inch from the edge, using a running stitch.

Using an iron, press the seam open on the wrong side of the work.

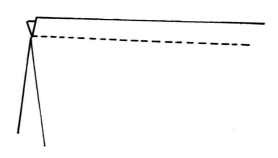

STEP 2

On the right side of the fabric, stitch along one side of the initial seam, sewing through both the top fabric and the seam allowance. Stitch ¼ inch from the seam. Adjust the length of stitches as desired for decorative effect.

STEP 3

Stitch a third seam, parallel to and on the opposite side of the initial seam.

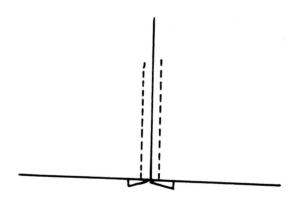

ON THE SEWING MACHINE

Certain sewing machines possess a very decorative triple running stitch.

Adjust the machine to this stitch.

Choose the stitch according to the effect you want: about ⅛ inch for a fine textile and up to ¼ inch for wool or thicker fabrics like denim.

Try out the triple stitch on a scrap of your fabric and adjust the thread tension so that the topstitching will not cause puckering of the material.

Use a synthetic thread of normal thickness. A thick thread runs the risk of giving the topstitching a "tamped down" appearance.

The Straight Skirt

The straight skirt is a classic piece in the world of sewing. With it you can practice scaling a pattern when you are just starting out in this technique. The model presented here can be fashioned in all sorts of fabrics. You can make warm winter skirts in tweed, flannel, wool, etc., or more spring-like skirts in cotton, linen, or real silk. Since it is practical and always in fashion, you will never tire of the straight skirt since you can adjust its length to coordinate with some of the other articles in the book, to suit current trends, or adjust to your own tastes.

YOU WILL NEED

Cotton pique, 40 inches by 54 inches wide

Flat grosgrain ribbon, 40 inches by 1 inch wide

Sewing thread, in a color that is darker or which sharply contrasts against the fabric

Basting thread, in a contrasting color

Extra-fine straight pins

Thimble, sized to fit your finger

Zipper, 7 inches in length, in a color matching the fabric

Hook and eye

Tailor's chalk

Dressmaker's scissors

MEASUREMENTS

Before choosing a pattern, take your measurements or those of the person for whom the garment is being made. For how to take these measurements, refer to page 247. You should always take measurements before choosing and purchasing a pattern.

You should also verify the sizing according to the source of the pattern, since the build and height can vary slightly from one country to another.

Moreover, it is important that you take measurements with great precision, if only to be able to compare them with those marked on the jacket of the pattern, its instructions, or its description.

So do not hesitate to get help and to proceed in a systematic fashion. To do this, dress only in your undergarments, keep your shoes on, and tie a thin ribbon around your waist to locate it during the measuring session. Keep the ribbon as horizontal as possible the entire time.

Stand straight and tall, with your arms at your sides and do not constrict the part of your body being measured with the tape measure.

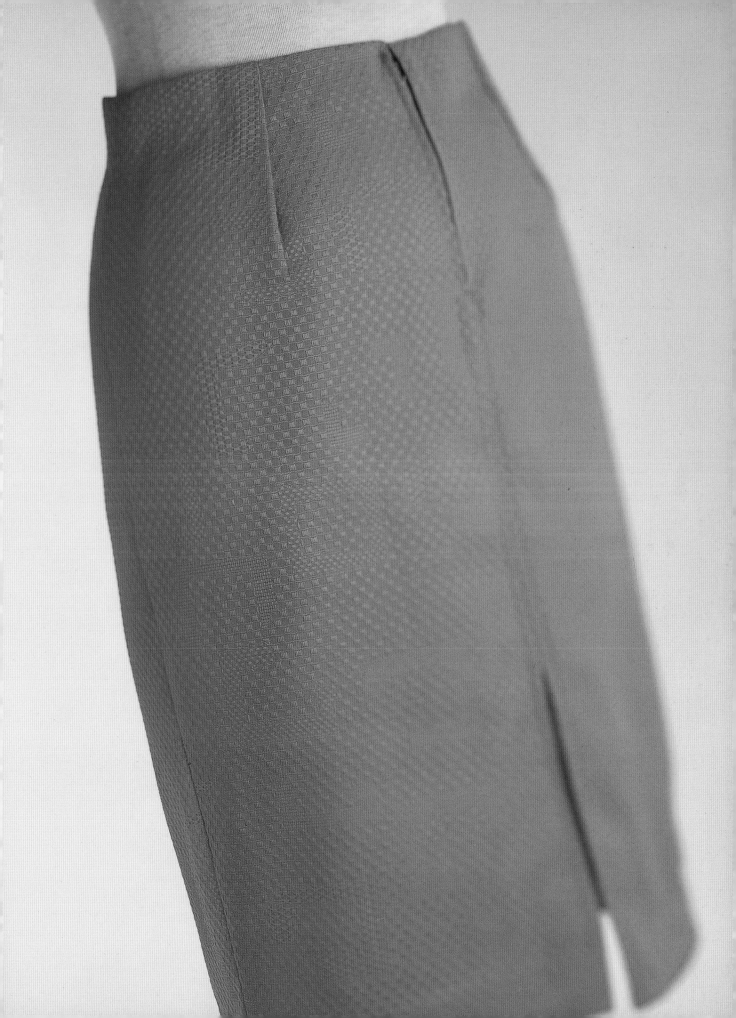

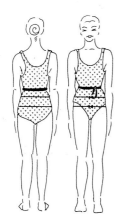

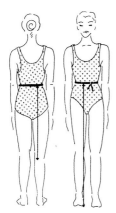

Measuring the Skirt Waist and Hips

The waist measurement corresponds to the length of the ribbon placed around the waist.

The hip measurement is taken in two places. First of all take the high hip measurement, which corresponds to the circumference just on top of the hip bones, then measure the full hips, situated at the fullest point of the buttocks.

Measuring the Skirt Length

The skirt length is taken from the waist to the crook of the knee (for a standard model).

The center back length is taken from the cord at the waist to the ground (see above left). The center front length is taken from the cord at the waist to the ground.

The distance between the hemline and the ground will allow you to calculate the exact length you desire. Subtract this measurement from the calculation of the lengths taken from the waist to obtain the actual heights you desire.

FABRIC DIMENSIONS

Length of fabrics without direction, ½ inch wide = one skirt length + 2¾ inches for hems + ⅝ inch for waistline seam.

Length of fabrics with direction, 54 inches wide = one skirt length + 2¾ inches for hems + ⅝ inch for waistline seam + half of all these dimensions (stagger these pieces to cut them).

Length of fabrics with or without direction, 36 inches wide = two skirt lengths = 2¾ inches twice for hems + ⅝ inch twice for waistline seam.

THE PATTERN

Of course, the idea is to choose a pattern that either corresponds exactly to the size you desire, or that has lines and marks for several sizes. However, it may happen that you do not have a choice in the size, or that the pattern has the right measurements but needs a few alterations. For a skirt, two cases may present themselves.

If the Pattern is Too Short

Split the front and back pieces along a horizontal line trace out 4 inches from the bottom and perpendicular to the straight grain. Insert an additional strip of paper between the split edges of the pattern to add the extra length. With edges straight and evenly spaced apart, pin or tape the split edges in place along the added strip.

HELPFUL HINTS

What should you do when the pattern does not indicate the width of the seam allowances? In general the amounts that should be added to the pattern for seams are: ⅝ inch for most seams and 2 to 3 inches for the bottom hem.

Rectify the seam lines on the sides, trimming the excess paper.

If the Pattern is Too Long

Do not alter the fullness of the skirt. Trace a horizontal line perpendicular to the straight grain, 4 inches from the bottom of the pattern. Draw a second line above the first, at a distance equal to the amount to be subtracted in order to obtain the ideal skirt length.

Fold, placing the two lines against each other, and hold in place with pins or tape. Adjust the seam line on each side by trimming the excess paper.

Size 14 Skirt

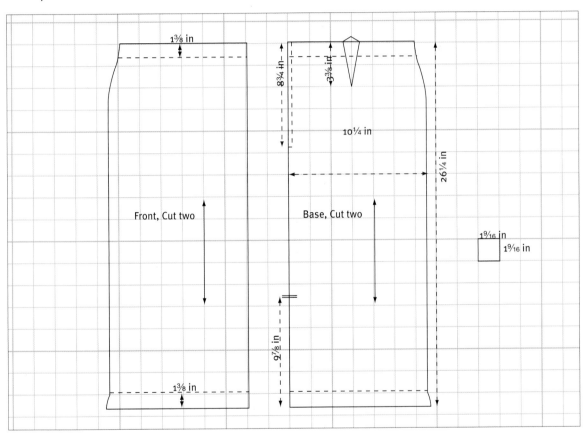

1⅜ in
8¾ in
3⅜ in
10¼ in
26¼ in
Front, Cut two
Base, Cut two
1⁹⁄₁₆ in
1⁹⁄₁₆ in
9⅞ in
1⅜ in

CUTTING THE FABRIC

Lay the pieces of the skirt on the wrong side of the fabric allowing space for seams and paying attention to the direction of the grain and of the motif, if there is one.

Pin the pattern to the fabric. Using tailor's chalk, trace out the outline of the pieces along the seam lines. Transfer the assembly marks indicated on the pattern as well.

Cut, taking into account the amount you will need for seam allowances. To make your life easier, mark these measurements as well before cutting.

THE STRAIGHT SKIRT IN 6 STEPS

After you have cut out the pieces, overcast their edges with a zigzag stitch. For assembly, design, attachment of the waistband, and finishing, follow the steps below.

1 ASSEMBLING THE FRONT AND BACK PIECES

With the right sides facing, pin the two back pieces together along the straight center edge and baste. Leaving 8¾ inches opening at the top and 10 inches at the bottom unsewn, stitch seam with a running stitch. Press the seam open with an iron. Topstitch on each side of the stitched section of the seam, using a thread in a darker color than the fabric, or one that contrasts sharply.

Place the right sides of the front pieces together, baste and stitch the entire center front seam. Press the seam open and top stitch as before.

2 FASHIONING THE BACK FINISHINGS

Continue the topstitched lines to the bottom on each side of the basted bottom of the back seam; remove the basting stitches to form a bottom slit.

At the top of the skirt, pin the darts. Stitch these starting at the edge of the waist of the skirt.

Do not make a backstitch at the end of each dart seam. Tie the two threads by hand and cut them ⅛ inch from the surface of the fabric.

Press the darts, turning them down toward the outer edge of the piece.

3 JOINING THE SIDES

Place the right sides of the front and back pieces against each other, pin and then baste the sides. Sew the two seams and press them open with an iron.

Topstitch, using the machine on the triple running stitch setting, as indicated in Step 1 (for a more detailed explanation of this stitch, see the three steps of The Double Topstitched Seam, explained with diagrams on pages 28–29).

ATTACHING THE ZIPPER

Center the zipper over basted opening at the top of the skirt with the zipper teeth 1¾ inches below the top edge. Install the zipper foot on the machine.

Stitch the zipper in place, ¼ inch from the basted opening edge and, at the bottom of the zipper, lift the presser foot, turn the piece to sew across the width of the zipper. Pivot the piece to sew the other side of the zipper. Remove the basting stitch.

ATTACHING THE WAISTBAND

Before attaching the grosgrain ribbon, you will need to reshape it. Soak it in water for a while, then iron it while still wet, stretching the bottom while you ease in the top. Let it dry, then try it on around the waist. The length of the grosgrain should be equal to the waist measurement + ½ or ¾ inch for ease. Cut off the excess.

Using tailor's chalk, mark the middle of the grosgrain ribbon, which should line up with the center front of the skirt. Baste it onto the skirt, 1½ inches from the top edge of the skirt. Pin together, then stitch.

FINISHING THE WAISTBAND

Double the extra 1½ inches of fabric above the waistband over the ribbon to cover it entirely, and iron into place.

Pin the three layers of the waistband together.

Stitch on the top of the skirt, ¼ inch from the edge, being sure to stitch through all three layers.

Close off the back of this fold along the zipper on the back part of the skirt with small slip stitches done by hand. Attach a hook and eye above the zipper (see page 109).

FINISHING

Try on the skirt to determine where the bottom hem should be. Mark the hem line, using tailor's chalk and a yard stick to help you. This hem line should be parallel to the ground and to the hipline. The line you obtain will not be on the straight grain; it will be rounded.

Take the skirt off and use an iron to turn the hem under, toward the inside of the skirt. Baste and try it on again, to ensure that the hem is properly formed all around.

Hem by hand, using a hemming stitch.

The Flat-fell Seam

PRELIMINARIES

The flat-fell seam is a flat, secure seam that is primarily used for sewing sportswear made out of quilted fabrics, such as fleece (polar knit).

There is another version of the flat-fell seam, called the mock flat-fell seam. This variant is mostly used on fine fabrics, but it can also be used for gathered pieces.

The basic method is the same for these two versions.

MORE ABOUT THE TECHNIQUE

The flat-fell seam is made in three steps, as explained in the outlined steps. The assembly of the pieces is all the simpler since no overcasting of the fabric edges is needed beforehand. Certain fabrics lend themselves better to this seam than others.

STEP 1

Place the two pieces of fabric edge to edge, with the right sides facing each other. Pin together, or baste.

Stitch ⅝ inch from the edges, being careful to keep the stitching quite straight and parallel to the bare cut of the fabric.

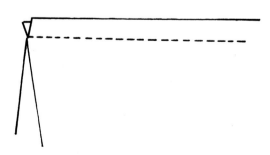

STEP 2

With the fabrics lying flat, trim one seam allowance to ¼ inch from the seam. Use the iron to turn under ¼ inch on the larger seam allowance as if you were forming a hem.

Press this hemmed seam allowance over the trimmed one. Pin together, or baste.

STEP 3

On top of the fabric, stitch parallel to and ⅛ inch from the fold, enclosing the raw edge of the trimmed seam allowance.

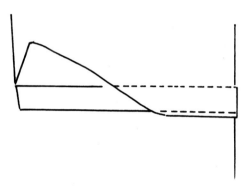

ON THE SEWING MACHINE

How do you knot off stitches? Begin by making 5 or 6 stitches, then push the reverse stitch button. The feed will move in the opposite direction, and the needle will restitch on top of the previous stitches.

Next, resume normal stitching. This process allows you to secure the stitches and to avoid having them come undone.

Repeat this process any time you come to the end of a stitching. Then cut the threads at the beginning and end of the seam, on the very edges of the fabric.

The Baby Bottle Cover

The baby bottle cover can be used to carry baby food when you are on the go, and can keep it warm while you are out. This cover can also be coordinated with the color scheme of the baby's room.

YOU WILL NEED

Loop pile fleece, 8 inches in orange

Regular fleece, 16 inches in apricot

Satin ribbon, 8 inches long

Sewing thread, in orange

Extra-fine pins

Drawing compass

Fine felt-tip pen, indelible

Yard stick

Dressmaker's scissors

MEASUREMENTS

Measure the height of the bottle and add 3¼ inches.

Measure the diameter of the bottle and add 1⅝ inches to this measurement.

FABRIC DIMENSIONS

Fleece is sold in a width of 58–60 inches. Therefore, depending on the bottle height, you can get two or three bottle slipcovers from this width.

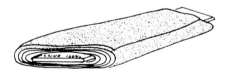

HELPFUL HINTS

Synthetic fleece is a light fabric that keeps heat well and has the advantage of being machine-washable. It is highly recommended for this project.

CUTTING THE FABRIC

Place the large rectangle and the round piece of the pattern on the back of the apricot-colored polar tricot, and the small rectangle on the back of the loop pile tricot.

Draw the outlines of the pieces with the felt-tip pen, remembering to transfer the assembly markings.

Cut the three pieces out, ⅝ inch from the trace marks.

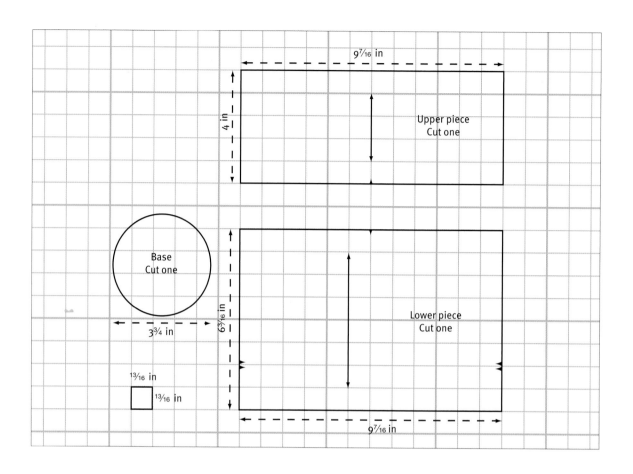

9⁷⁄₁₆ in

Upper piece
Cut one

4 in

Base
Cut one

3¾ in

6³⁄₁₆ in

Lower piece
Cut one

¹³⁄₁₆ in
¹³⁄₁₆ in

9⁷⁄₁₆ in

THE BABY BOTTLE COVER
IN 4 STEPS

This cover is practical, fun, and easy to put together, and makes an excellent gift for mother and newborn.

ASSEMBLING THE TWO PIECES

Place the small rectangle of fleece on the large one, edge to edge and with the right sides together.

Pin the pieces together and stitch along the trace line as evenly as possible.

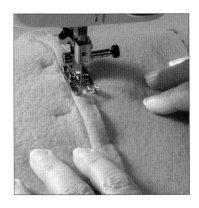

PREPARATION OF THE FLAT-FELL SEAM

Trim the seam allowance of the orange fleece to ¼ inch from the stitching. Fold down ¼ inch of the seam allowance for the apricot fleece, and fold it over the one that was previously cut.

Pin the layers together.

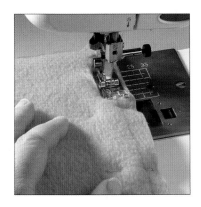

SEWING THE BACK

On the right side of the fabric, stitch the top of the flat-fell seam. Next refold the body of the cover, marker to marker, with the right sides of the fabric facing.

Pin together, then stitch.

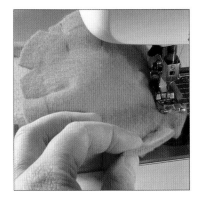

ASSEMBLING THE BASE OF THE SLIPCOVER

Pin the base, trim the seam allowances to ¼ inch and notch the rounded edges of the circle.

Make two successive stitches on the trace line to give more solidity to the assembly.

FINISHING

At the top of the cover, make a double fold of ¾ inch and press it in place. Finish it off using a straight stitch on the machine, or sew it by hand with a hemming stitch.

Tie a ribbon above the bottle to close the cover.

The French Seam

PRELIMINARIES

The double seam, called the French seam, is recommended for the assembly of transparent and light fabrics, and, in general, for fabrics that will be washed often, like cotton or organdy.

There are two advantages to using the French seam:

- It gives a clean, flat seam, with no unraveling or overcasting, and is ideal for fine fabrics;
- It is a very secure seam when used on any fabric.

MORE ABOUT THE TECHNIQUE

The French seam is made in two steps. The first step consists of making a plain seam on the right side of the pieces of fabric, and in the second step the first seam is covered, making it invisible.

STEP 1

Place the pieces of fabric edge to edge, with the wrong sides together. Pin together or baste, depending on which you prefer.

Stitch ¼ inch from the edges.

Trim the edges of the fabric (or the seam allowances) ⅛ inch from the stitching you have just done.

Press the seam without opening it; simply turn it to one side.

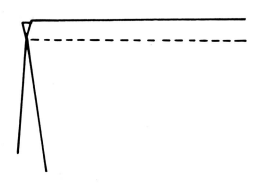

The edge of the first seam must be carefully cut, to prevent it from unraveling through the second seam.

The pressing of the first seam is important: It should be done such to obtain a very flat, even seam. For a nice finish, maintain an even spacing between the two stitchings.

A DRESSMAKER'S TRICK

If the fabric does not move freely over the feed teeth and is preventing you from guiding the assembly smoothly through the machine, place a piece of white tissue paper or a thin sheet of artist's tracing paper between the teeth of the machine and the fabric and adjust the length of the stitch to a scant ⅛ inch.

When the work is complete, remove the paper.

Adjust the machine to the triple elastic stitch (also called overlock stitch), and set the width of the stitch to zero: "0." In this way, the stitches will be straight and will maintain a great elasticity, which will prevent the fabric from puckering. The only inconvenience is that, if you make a mistake these stitches cannot be undone.

STEP 2

Turn the fabric onto the wrong side, so that the right sides of it are facing each other.

Press to flatten the stitching along its length, and pin.

Stitch ³⁄₁₆ inch from the folded edge.

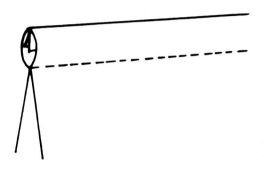

ON THE SEWING MACHINE

The assembly of thin, transparent fabrics can be delicate work, since the stitches can cause the fabric to pucker. Or, it could happen that threads are left hanging loose after stitching.

The solution is to check certain details and to carefully adjust the sewing machine. To do this:

— Install a new, fine needle (size 70) so you are not working with a blunt point;

— Use a fine embroidery thread, either synthetic or twisted (size 30 or 50; you can find this at DMC, for example);

— Install a metallic Teflon-coated presser foot (if your machine has one) or if you do not have one, a roller foot or a even-feed foot;

— Do a test run using the same fabric as the one you are working with to adjust the spool and bobbin tensions. If the fabric puckers under the stitches, lessen the tension. If the stitches are loose, increase the tension in the thread.

The Striped Casement Curtain

A casement curtain hanging in front of a window should be freely moving and gauzy, to lend a certain fluid harmony to the room. The play of stripes on this piece is affected by the successive joining of bands of organdy in three different colors.

YOU WILL NEED

Cotton organdy, in blue, anise and ecru (dimensions to be determined based on the instructions for the method being used)
Bobbin with imitation cotton or with DMC Broder Special (No. 30 or 50), in ecru
Extra-fine pins
Yardstick
Dressmaker's scissors

HELPFUL HINTS

If you choose to suspend the curtain with tabs, subtract the finished length of these tabs from the length calculation for the curtain. If you would like to have the curtain go all the way to the floor, subtract ⅝ inch from the calculated length, so that the piece does not drag against the floor.

MEASUREMENTS

The length calculation for a casement curtain is the same for any type of window. For you to take accurate measurements, the curtain rod should be installed on its supports.

The Curtain Length

Measure from the top of the curtain rod to the bottom of where you want the curtain to fall. Add to this measurement the length of the heading of the curtain and the length of the hem (in general, this is at least 2 inches).

The Curtain Width

For a freely moving casement curtain, make the width of the curtain two and a half times the length of the curtain rod. If you would like the curtain to be more gathered, take three times the length of the rod and in either case add 2 inches for the side hems.

FABRIC DIMENSIONS

Fabrics for making casement curtains come in wide widths from 60 inches to 94 inches.

If possible, plan it so that the selvages of the fabrics you choose will match up with the sides of the curtain.

If the width of your curtain is less than the width of the fabric (including the selvages), only buy one curtain length (for the calculation of the measurements, see above).

If the width of your curtain is more than that of the total width of the fabric, calculate how many strips you will need to get the width you would like to have for the curtain. Then, to get the dimensions, multiply one curtain length by the number of fabric strips you need (same calculation as before).

The Number of Suspension Tabs

When you have a simple wooden or brass curtain rod, you can suspend your casement curtain with tabs.

The spacing between the tabs should be in uniform intervals of 4½ to 6 inches; anything greater than these dimensions, the curtain runs the risk of gaping. Calculate the number of tabs you will need by dividing the width of the unfinished curtain by various measurements within that range to find whichever spacing gives you a whole number of straps. The first and last tabs are to be attached to the right and left edges of the curtain.

CUTTING THE FABRIC

Remove the selvages, then cut as many strips of the blue- and ecru-colored organdy as you would like, making each band 8¼ inches in width, and adding 4⅝ inches for heading and hems. Next, cut as many 14¼-inch strips of the anise-colored organdy as needed.

Finally, cut another strip of the ecru-colored organdy for making the tabs. This strip should be 8¼ inches wide.

THE STRIPED CASEMENT CURTAIN IN 4 STEPS

The strips of color are arranged as follows: In alternating strips of anise-, blue- and ecru-colored organdy. This motif is repeated throughout the width of the curtain. Begin and end the panel with an anise-colored strip.

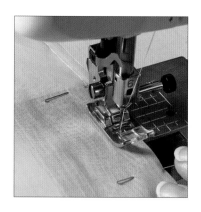

1 ASSEMBLING THE STRIPS

Position a blue strip and an anise strip with the wrong sides together and edges matching; pin the two layers together. Execute a French seam along one edge of these strips (for details on the technique, see pages 42–43).

Pin an ecru strip to the other side of the blue strip and attach these two pieces with another French seam, as before.

Continue to add one strip of color at a time, taking care to follow the same pattern (anise, blue, ecru).

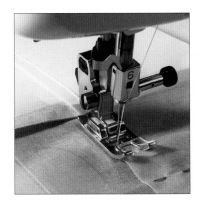

MAKING THE HEMS

Once you have the desired curtain width, press a fold of ⅜ inch on each side of the curtain with an iron. Over this first fold, form a second one of ⅝ inch, and pin the layers together. Stitch the hems ⅜ inch from the edge.

On the top and the bottom of the curtain, turn up ¾ inch of fabric. Use an iron to fold up a further hem of 1½ inches on the top and 2⅜ inches on the bottom.

Adjust the machine to the running stitch with a length of ⅛ inch. Stitch each hem ⅜ inch from its inner fold edge.

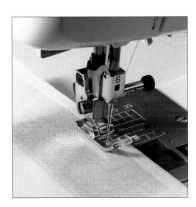

MAKING THE TABS

Cut out the desired number of tabs from the remaining strip of ecru, making each tab 15¾ inches long by 8¼ inches wide. Fold each tab in half lengthwise to make a strip 4⅛ inches wide. Sew a French seam along the edge.

Turn the tabs right side out, centering the seam on one side. Fold ⅜ inch of the ends in toward the interior of the tabs and stitch closed. Fold tab in half, end to end to form a loop 7⅞ inches long. Pin ends together.

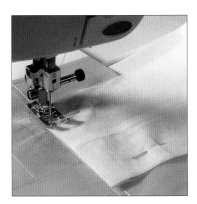

ATTACHING THE TABS

Using pins, mark the attachment point of each tab on the top hem of the casement curtain.

Line up the middle point along the width of each tab with the point marked out by the pin. Pin the tab ends onto the head of the curtain.

Using a straight stitch, sew the bottoms of the suspension tabs along the previous stitching line on the heading of the curtain.

Attach the tabs all along the top of the curtain, stitching ⅜ inch from the edge.

FINISHING

Carefully press your work, using starch if necessary.

Pass the curtain rod through the tabs of the curtain, then attach the rod to the supports previously installed for this purpose.

Note that organdy needs to be lightly starched after each washing.

Sewing on the Bias

Working on the bias of a fabric requires much precision when you are cutting and assembling a piece. It is necessary to avoid stretching the seams during assembly.

This technique particularly lends itself to making dirndl skirts, jackets or blouses with raglan sleeves.

This method has two basic underlying principles to it.

· Marking the bias:

The first thing you have to do is mark out the bias of your fabric.

· Sewing on the bias:

For assembly, use the plain seam; this is the recommendation given in numerous clothing or decorative projects.

MORE ABOUT THE TECHNIQUE

Sewing on the bias, if carefully done, will let you neatly join together pieces that have other than rectilinear shapes. Fabrics prepared and cut in this manner offer an advantageous suppleness, which greatly facilitates assembly and finishing.

STEP 1

Place the fabrics edge to edge, with the right sides facing each other. Pin them together, or baste.

Carefully stitch ⅝ inch from the edge.

STEP 2

Use the tip of the iron to open this seam.

STEP 3

Overcast the edges of the seam allowances with a zigzag stitch. Make the stitch wide and long.

MARKING THE BIAS

If the fabric you are working with is a simple weave, the warp and weft threads cross each other perpendicularly. To find the bias, fold the fabric so that the width is superimposed on the length.

Once folded, the fabric forms a 45-degree angle. Using the tailor's chalk, trace a line along the longest side of this triangle.

Other ways of doing this include forming a crease by ironing, or placing pins as markers along this line. Choose the method you will use based on the nature of your fabric.

Use a plastic triangle to check the 45-degree angle. The cutting edges of the pattern should be placed parallel to the line of bias.

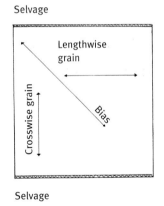

ON THE SEWING MACHINE

For making a straight seam without doing a basting stitch beforehand, follow to the guiding lines engraved on the guide plate situated under the presser foot of the machine.

With the piece to the left and the seam allowance held in place to the right of the presser foot, the edge of the fabric should line up with one of the grooved lines of the plate. These lines usually are ¼ inch apart.

If the width of the seam allowance passes the last line on the plate, use a piece of colored tape set at the right distance and parallel to the lines to guide you.

The Lamp Shade

The goal of this project is to give new life to a worn-out lamp shade. For this you must use a 100% cotton or silk fabric, and the bulb used should not be more than 40 watts. Do not strip the old shade from the frame, since it will help to guide you when you are setting up the new shade.

YOU WILL NEED

Striped fabrics, remnants or scraps of material
Pre-folded cotton bias binding, ⅞ inch wide, in a color that coordinates with the fabrics
Cotton sewing thread, for the machine, in a color that matches the fabrics
Extra-fine pins
Brown wrapping paper, in a large sheet
A sturdy sewing needle
Thimble, sized to fit your finger
Drawing pencil
Plastic triangle
Fabric glue
Clothespins
Tailor's chalk
Dressmaker's scissors

MEASUREMENTS

For a standard, conical lamp shade, use the drawing pencil and the plastic triangle to trace a straight line from the top to the bottom of the lamp shade.

Place a sheet of brown wrapping paper on a table. Tape the corners of the paper to the table.

Place the lamp shade frame on the paper, with the line you marked with the pencil against the paper. Mark the position of this line on the paper.

Slowly roll the frame on the paper as you trace out the arcs that the shade makes as you are rolling it. Continue in this way to make a complete turn of the shade.

Cut the pattern along this trace line and verify that your pattern completely covers the lamp shade.

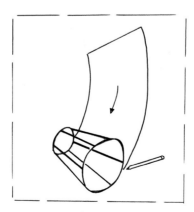

Rolling the lamp shade frame along the brown wrapping paper

HELPFUL HINTS

Prefolded bias binding is very easy to use. You can find it in a notions store in the form of precut strips whose folds have been set with an iron. All you need to do is select the width you desire, in a color matching the fabric you are using. Attaching it is easy; if you are short on time and your project allows for it, it is the ideal solution.

FABRIC DIMENSIONS

If the pattern fits within the whole width of the fabric with at least 2 inches to spare on each end, you will only need a length of fabric equal to the height of the arc pattern from the lowest to the highest point + 4 inches.

CUTTING THE FABRIC

Fold your arc pattern in half and then half again, to mark out four quadrants. Number these pieces.

Fold the edges of the fabric in such a manner as to find the bias.

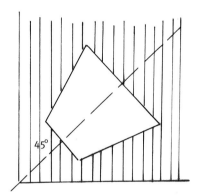

45°

A quarter of the pattern placed on the bias of the fabric

Lay the four pieces of the pattern on the fabric, taking care to align the top of each piece against a particular stripe, so that when joined, the stripes will line up. Pin the patterns in place, and trace the outline of each piece with tailor's chalk. Cut out each fabric piece 2¾ inches beyond the trace mark.

THE BIAS

This project has been done with prefolded bias binding, which is easy to use (see the box above). For projects that are more delicate, or that require the subtle coordination of color and texture, you also have the option of crafting your own bias binding from the fabric of your choice.

Refer to page 222 for some more helpful hints and suggestions that will show you how to cut and attach such a bias binding.

THE LAMP SHADE
IN 6 STEPS

One of the advantages of sewing on the bias is the great elasticity that the fabric has when it is cut in this manner. For this project, cutting the fabric on the bias makes the piece adjust perfectly to the conical shape of the lamp shade.

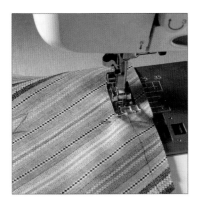

ASSEMBLING THE PIECES

With the right sides of the fabric against each other, pin piece 1 onto piece 2 along one of its sides.

Proceeding in the same fashion, pin piece 3 onto piece 2, and finally piece 4 to piece 3.

SEWING THE PIECES TOGETHER

After you have tested the stitch on a scrap of the fabric you are using (or a similar one), stitch the pieces together using a running stitch.

Assemble the four pieces.

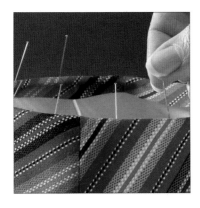

DRESSING THE LAMP SHADE

With the right sides of the fabric against each other, pin and then sew piece 1 to piece 4, and press open the seams with an iron. Cut back the seam allowances to within ⅜ inch of the seam, and then turn the work over onto its right side.

Now, slide your assembled shade onto the lamp shade frame over the old shade. Fold the top and bottom edges in toward the inside of the frame. Pin to keep the ensemble in place.

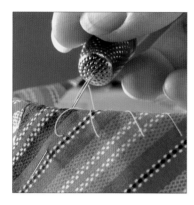

4 SEWING THE EDGES OF THE SHADE

Using a needle and thread, hand-sew around the circumference of the frame with a large hem stitch, stitching through the fabric of the shade and over the frame. Use a thimble to help you push the needle through the thickness of the material on the old lamp shade.

Pull the fabric tight over the frame (without overstretching it) and secure the top and bottom edges of the new shade.

5 ATTACHING THE FIRST PART OF THE BIAS BINDING

Cut off the excess fabric from the upper fold at the top of the piece.

Place a thread of glue along one of the sides and on the back of the bias binding. Position the bias binding on the edge, and let it dry.

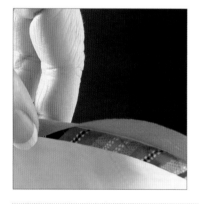

6 ATTACHING THE SECOND PART OF THE BIAS BINDING

Now put some glue on the second side of the bias binding and fold it over toward the inside of the lamp shade.

Use a few clothespins to hold the binding in place while it is drying.

Attach the bias binding to the lower edge in the same manner.

FINISHING

Avoid leaving the clothespins in place longer than is necessary, to prevent their leaving marks on the fabric.

If the fabric you have chosen for the shade dressing is thin or light-colored, avoid using wooden clothespins, which can leave marks.

Alternatively, you can use other things to hold the cloth in place, such as hairpins.

Sewing Mitered Corners

PRELIMINARIES

Mitering is a technique that gives you the option of marrying together contrasting fabrics, or pieces of cloth cut from the same type of fabric, but in different colors.

These mitered corners give your work an air of elegance and style. This is why, in addition to the fact that these kinds of projects are well suited to it, this technique is often used to decorate tablecloths, table napkins, cushions, curtains, sheet sets, and the like.

MORE ABOUT THE TECHNIQUE

Putting together a mitered corner requires some skill, and so the steps outlined opposite should be followed with precision. This technique, in addition to giving an immaculate finish to corners, allows you infinite customizing possibilities. You can play with coordinating colors and textures, the width of the strips, and the borders . . . it is all up to you.

STEP 1

On the back of the fabric, trace out a square or rectangle to match the shape of the table top. Cut ⅝ inch beyond the trace marks.

Trace out two strips to match the length and two strips to match the width of the traced center piece. At each end of each strip, trace in additional length that is twice the desired width of the *finished* border.

Cut ⅝ inch from the outer trace marks.

STEP 2

Fold each strip in half lengthwise and press this fold line, or baste the centerline of each strip. On each end of opened strip, trace a 90-degree angle; the marked centerline should bisect the angle to form a 45-degree angle on each side. Cut off the excess fabric ⅝ inch from the traced angle (if desired, leave a little extra to allow for adjustments).

You should be very rigorous in taking measurements in order to assure the angles are precise. If you are at all unsure, make the strips a little longer, sew them and then readjust them, to make them sit well in the corner of the central piece. Retrace the points using a plastic triangle after they have been definitively assembled.

A DRESSMAKER'S TRICK

If you do not wish to play with the contrast between two different fabrics but yet would like to put an elegant finishing on the borders of table napkins, sheets or curtains, you can also use the Mitered Hem technique to produce immaculate corners. See page 57 for the two possible methods.

STEP 3

Mark the midpoints of each side of the central piece, as well as the midpoint of each strip.

Right sides facing, pin the strips to the central piece by aligning these marks.

STEP 4

Stitch these strips ⅝ inch from the edges. Stop the stitch at each corner of the central piece, then start a new line of stitching on the other side of the corner.

Carefully press the seams open with an iron.

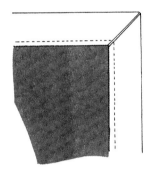

STEP 5

With the right sides of the fabric against each other, pin the corresponding sides of the two points face to face.

Stitch from the edge of the corner of the central piece, heading toward the point of the strip. Leave the needle stuck in the fabric and reorient the piece in such a way so that you can finish the seam on the other part of the point (see "On The Sewing Machine" below).

Complete all four corners in this fashion.

ON THE SEWING MACHINE

How can you master making a seam at a corner? To do this, leave the needle stuck in the corner. Raise the presser foot, and then make a quarter turn with the fabric. Lower the presser foot, and finish stitching in this new direction.

Press the seam open with an iron and remove the excess fabric. The amount of fabric you need to cut off will depend on the nature of the material you are using. However, take care not to cause unraveling by cutting too close to a seam.

THE MITERED HEM

This type of hem is often used in decorative work. The mitering can be done in different ways, depending on the length of the hem and the height of the furnishing.

1. The Unsewn Miter

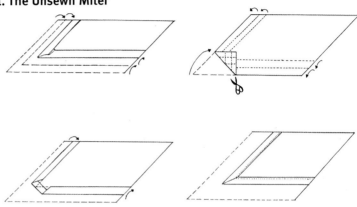

This method is reserved for hems that are not in excess of 1½ inches deep. The miter is made from a series of folds.

Mark the size of the hem with a basting thread. Fold, using the iron to mark the crease well.

Unfold the turned-in edges and refold the corner on the diagonal. Notch the corner and fold it anew, following the pressing marks

Hem by hand or on the machine, using a hemming stitch.

2. The Sewn Miter

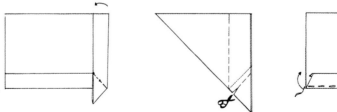

This method is suited to large hems and to heavier or thicker textiles.

Press to mark the folds of the hem. Fold the fabric with the right sides facing. Pin the corner diagonally, and stitch it along this line.

Cut off the excess fabric in the corner, ⅜ inch from the seam. Press the seam open with an iron. Turn the hem to the back of the piece. Press and turn in ⅜ inch on the edge of the hem. Stitch, or hem by hand, using a hemming stitch.

The Square Tablecloth

Using the mitering technique makes it possible for you to join two different fabrics together and to obtain a very refined and aesthetically pleasing product. This type of edging is also recommended for enlarging the dimensions of a work, like a plaid, a bedspread, or the flap of a flat sheet.

YOU WILL NEED

Floral print fabric, square, at least 50 inches wide

Striped fabrics, 2⅜ yard by 62 inches, with length-wise stripes

Sewing thread, in a color to match the fabrics

Basting thread, in a contrasting color

Extra-fine pins

Plastic triangle

Tailor's chalk

Dressmaker's scissors

HELPFUL HINTS

You can execute the finishing of a tablecloth by hand or on the machine. If using the machine, work on the top of the tablecloth; if you are finishing by hand, work on the wrong side of the piece.

MEASUREMENTS

For a **simple tablecloth** with a drop that falls to about mid-way between the tabletop and the ground:

Tablecloth length = length of the tabletop + 27½ inches or 13¾ inches for each drop + 4 inches for the hems.

Tablecloth width = width of the tabletop + 27½ inches for the total drop length + 4 inches for the hems.

For a **formal tablecloth** with a drop length all the way to the floor:

Tablecloth length = length of the tabletop + twice the height from the tabletop to the floor + 4 inches for the hems.

Tablecloth width = width of the tabletop + twice the height from the tabletop to the floor + 4 inches for the hems.

Table napkins in general are square; their size depends on the type of service for which they are to be used.

Tea napkins: These range in size from 10 inches x 10 inches to 16 inches x 16 inches.

Dinner napkins: These range from 16 inches x 16 inches to 24 inches x 24 inches.

FABRIC DIMENSIONS

In this project, the tablecloth falls to a good midlength. Therefore the borders need to be wide.

Plan for at least 8 inches of width for the finished borders, as well as a length corresponding to the dimensions of your tabletop + 8 inches all around for the drop. The length of the strips will be the length of your central piece + 16 inches of width (for twice the 8-inch-wide finished strips).

CUTTING THE FABRIC

Cut a square with sides 50 inches from the floral print.

On the wrong side of the striped fabric, trace out four strips whose ends are pointed (see the pattern below).

Cut these four pieces out, ⅝ inch from the trace marks.

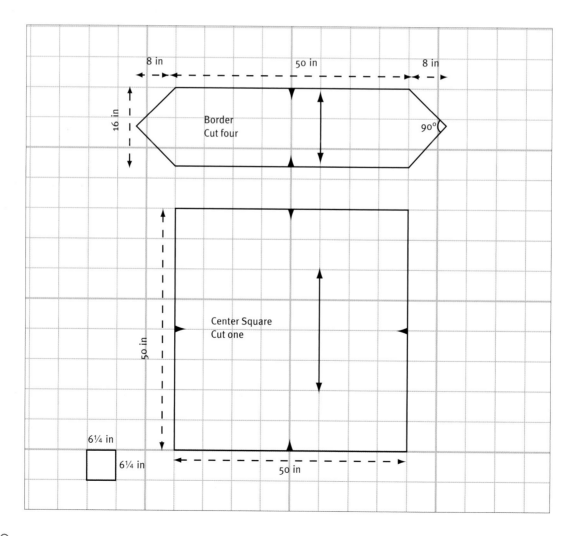

THE SQUARE TABLECLOTH
IN 4 STEPS

Overcast the edges of the pieces. With the aid of a basting thread (or iron), mark the centerline along each strip. Mark the midpoint of each side of the central piece, as well as the midpoint of each strip. With right sides facing, pin the strips to the central piece, matching midpoint.

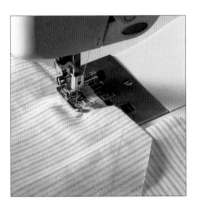

1 JOINING THE STRIPS TO THE CENTRAL SQUARE

Stitch the strips ⅝ inch from the edges, leaving seam allowances at the corners unsewn.

On the central piece, stop the stitch at each corner, pivot, then begin a new stitching on the other side of each corner, adding the next strip.

Press the seams open, taking care not to deform the corners thus formed.

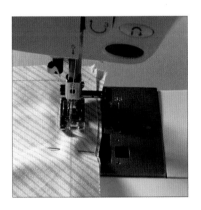

2 MAKING MITERED POINTS

With the right sides of the border fabric against each other, pin the corresponding sides of the two points face to face. Stitch from the edge on the corner of the central piece, heading toward the point of the strip.

Leave the needle stuck in the fabric and reorient the piece in a way so that you can finish the seam on the other part of the point.

Repeat this process for all four corners.

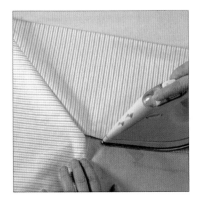

3 PREPARING THE BACK PART OF MITERED STRIPS

Press the seams of the points open with an iron. Trim the points of the corners to prevent any puckering.

Cut the seam allowances to ⅜ inch.

Use the iron to form the fold for the hem, using the basting line in the middle as a guide. Be precise. Then, turn down half of each strip toward the wrong side of the piece.

ATTACHING THE STRIPS TO THE BACK OF THE PIECE

On the reverse side of the tablecloth, fold under ⅝ inch along the free edge of the border strips, and baste to the stitching line of the assembled piece, covering the line.

FINISHING

Two finishes are possible:
— On the top of the tablecloth, machine stitch the layers of the mitered strip ⅜ inch from the edge of the central piece.
— On the underside of the piece, hand-sew the edge of the band onto the side of the central piece, using a hemming stitch.

3

ROUNDED AND GATHERED FORMS

Working with a Rounded Form

PRELIMINARIES

In sewing, you encounter rounded edges when assembling sleeves and arm-holes, the necklines of certain types of blouses, or the crotches of shorts or trousers.

There are several other instances when you may have to work with rounded parts, and we are going to study the various techniques involved in handling them. All these types of assembly need your care and attention. You should plan to work carefully and to take your time.

MORE ABOUT THE TECHNIQUE

When faced with having to assemble two concave pieces, two convex pieces, or a convex piece to a concave one, the important thing is to maintain the suppleness and evenness of the assembly: Suppleness, because you want to avoid puckers or the for-mation of embarrassing creases, and evenness for the width of the turned-under edges and the seam allowances.

STEP 1

Pin the right sides of the two pieces of fabrics against each other. If the two pieces have different shapes, for instance one is round and the other straight, place the rounded form on the straight one.

Pin together, or baste.

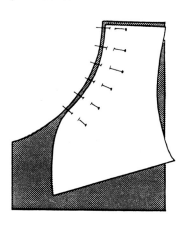

STEP 2

Stitch ⅝ inch from the edge.

STEP 3

Using the dressmaker's scissors, notch the seams at 1¼-inch intervals, where the form is the most curved.

Overcast the edges of these seam allowances.

STEP 4

Open the seam on the side of the straight piece using the point of the iron. If the two pieces have the same amount of curvature, press the seam on one side.

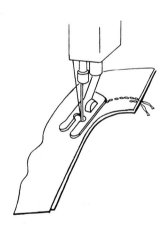

ON THE SEWING MACHINE

In order to obtain a nice rounded seam, adjust the sewing speed to "slowest." Turn the fabric little by little, allowing it to "come through" without your pushing it under the feed.

If the curvature of the piece is too deep to facilitate this, stop the stitching with the needle still stuck in the fabric, raise the presser foot, and realign the piece in the direction of the curve.

Lower the presser foot and resume stitching.

NOTCHES, CLIPPING, AND TRIMMING

After stitching curved seams, the edges are often cut to allow ease or remove excess fabric so the seam will lie flat and appear smooth on the right side.

Clipping

Curved edges that are rounded inward as they are sewn receive small straight cuts or clips that allow the fabric to stretch around the curve, which rounds outward when the piece is turned.

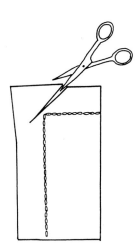

Trimming

Corners are trimmed to remove excess fabric when the piece is turned right side out (see diagram above).

Seam allowances may also be trimmed close to the stitching line to give ease to the seam.

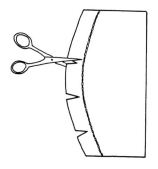

Notches

Small wedges are cut from curves that round outward to remove excess fabric that would buckle up when the piece is turned right side out to form the higher inward curved edge.

The Bolster

This type of cushion is an excellent item to introduce you to the assembly of rounded forms. The assembly of a rounded piece onto a straight one is, in effect, relatively easy to do, in comparison to the crafting of pieces such as toys and rag dolls, round cushions, or even certain bags like drawstring bags, whose creation is clearly more complex.

YOU WILL NEED

Silk cloth, in dimensions based on the size of the bolster

Sewing thread, in a color that matches the fabric

Fine pins

Brown wrapping paper, in a large sheet

One zipper, about 2½ inches shorter than the length of the bolster, in a color that matches the fabric

Two tassels, for trimming

Drawing compass

Drawing pencil

Plastic triangle

Yardstick

Dressmaker's scissors

MEASUREMENTS

Measure the length and the diameter of the bolster.

Multiply the diameter by 3.14 in order to determine the fabric width needed to cover the bolster.

Add 1⅝ inches to these measurements for the seam allowances.

FABRIC DIMENSIONS

If the whole width of the fabric (including the selvage) is sufficient to cover the width of the bolster + diameter of the end + 3½ inches, the length necessary is to equal the length of the bolster + 1⅝ inches.

If the width of the bolster + diameter of end + 3½ inches exceeds the width of the fabric, the length necessary is equal to the length of the bolster + the diameter of the end + 3½ inches.

HELPFUL HINTS

The silk cloth used for this model is very nice, but sometimes it can be delicate to work with. To avoid the risk of puckering the fabric, install the Teflon foot and a fine needle. Use a thread that is fine enough for the material, and stitch using the straight stitch or the zigzag stitch.

THE PATTERN

On the brown wrapping paper, draw a rectangle in the dimensions of the slipcover of the bolster.

Draw a circle with the diameter of the bolster on the paper as well, which will be used to cut out two circles of fabric for the ends.

Cut these two shapes out along the trace lines. Later, when you are cutting the fabric, you will take the seam allowances into account, both for the rectangle and the two end circles.

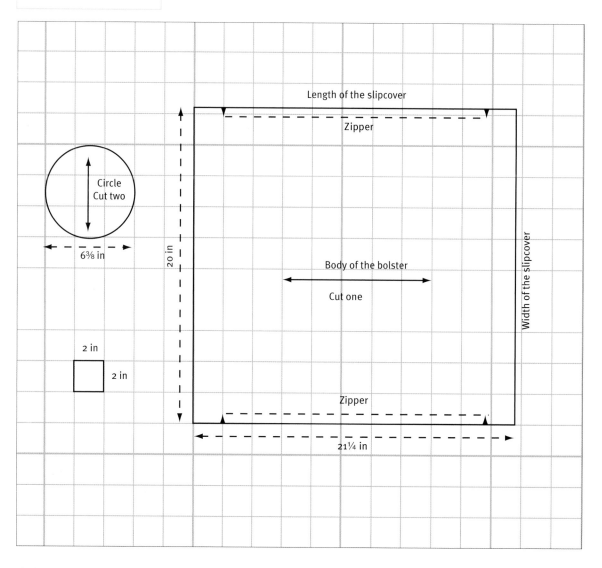

CUTTING THE FABRIC

Place the paper rectangle on the wrong side of the fabric. Pin the paper and the fabric together. Use tailor's chalk to trace the outline of the pieces onto the cloth. Cut ¾ inch from the trace line.

Fold the rest of the cloth in half with right sides together. Lay the paper circle on the fabric. Pin, and then use tailor's chalk to trace the outline of the pieces onto the cloth. Cut ¾ inch from the trace marks.

You will thus have two similar circles of fabric. These circles, when assembled, will give the bolster its shape.

A zipper installed along the length of the slipcover will allow you to remove it easily from the bolster.

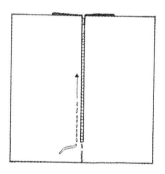

THE BOLSTER IN 4 STEPS

As previously indicated in the details on the technique for "Working with a Rounded Form," do not overcast the edges of curved pieces before you have finished the assembly of this work to avoid distorting the curves.

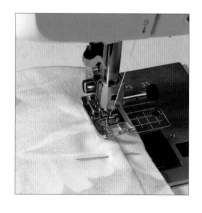

1 FORMING THE CYLINDER OF THE BOLSTER

Fold the fabric in half along its width, right sides facing in, and pin the long edges together.

Stitch along the trace line at each end of the long edge for 1¼ inches, leaving a center zipper opening. Press seam open, forming folds along the opening. Pin the zipper along the opening and baste it in place.

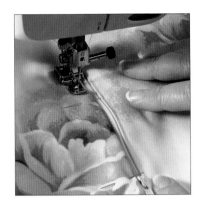

ATTACHING THE ZIPPER

Turn the garment over onto its right side and install the zipper foot. Stitch ⅛ inch from the teeth of the zipper.

Reinforce the seam with a few backstitches, done by hand, at the ends of the opening. Leave the zipper open throughout the assembly stages.

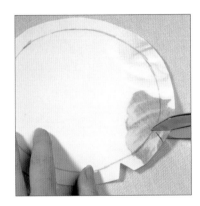

SETTING IN THE END CIRCLES OF THE BOLSTER

Notch the border of the cloth circles; cut notches ⅜ inch deep every 1¼ inches.

With the right sides together, baste the two end circles to the body of the cushion.

At this stage, the edges of the circle have not yet been overcast.

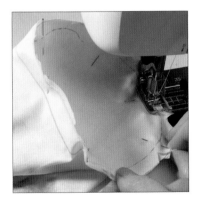

JOINING THE CIRCLES TO THE BODY OF THE BOLSTER

Stitch along the trace marks you made previously.

Press the seam allowances toward the flat part of the body of the bolster and overcast.

Turn the slipcover right side out. Attach a tassel to the center of each circle using a few back stitches.

FINISHING

When pressing, thread the open slipcover over a sleeve board (see page 246) in order to preserve the fullness of the piece and to avoid making any undesirable creases.

Square or Rectangular Forms

PRELIMINARIES

This type of assembly is often used in decorative sewing, in making certain cushions, seat covers, garment dust covers, and poufs or bench dressings with a foam seat.

This technique requires close attention to detail when taking measurements and when cutting the pieces out, but these precautions are necessary if you want to obtain a nice, clean finish to your project.

MORE ABOUT THE TECHNIQUE

To illustrate this technique, we will be studying the bench cushion mounted on a block of foam. This basic example will allow you to grasp the general principle of working on square or rectangular forms, which you can then adapt to other sorts of projects.

STEP 1

Cut the bands that will form the sides of the bench from the length of the fabric.

Attach a zipper to one of these pieces.

STEP 2

With the right sides of the fabric together, pin each of the four bands to the edges of the "top/bottom" piece.

Stitch ⅝ inch from the edges, leaving seam allowance at the corners unattached; press the seams open with an iron.

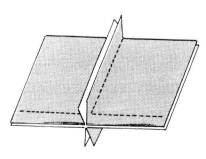

STEP 3

Stitch the widths of the bands to one another at each corner to form the box. Press the seams open with an iron and turn the piece inside out.

STEP 4

Slide the assembled unit on the foam block. If necessary, adjust the seams along the width of the four bands.

STEP 5

Turn the piece wrong side out again. Matching corners, pin the second "top/bottom" piece on the assembled part.

Stitch ⅝ inch from the edge, leaving an opening for turning.

STEP 6

Press the seams open, clip the corners, and trim the seam allowances to ⅜ inch. Overcast the edges of the pieces with a zigzag stitch. Turn the piece to the right side.

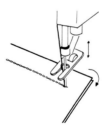

ON THE SEWING MACHINE

A piece that must withstand a lot of tension during assembly, finishing, or in its ultimate use must be tailored from a resistant fabric and have seams that can withstand any test. For a bench cushion, you should use a sturdy drapery thread.

You can also consolidate the work by making two parallel seams side by side at each stage in the assembly. Set the stitch length to ⅛ inch and stitch.

The Padded Cushion

The mattresses on our beds are crafted in the same manner as the cushion described here. The only difference is that the smaller size of this cushion makes it easier to work with. This model requires as much hand work (for finishing) as machine. Using this technique, you can make a padded headboard, a seat cushion, a beach mattress, and many other things.

YOU WILL NEED

Damask mattress cloth, 1⅛ yard by 44 inches in width, in pink
Synthetic stuffing, about 50 ounces
Sewing thread, in a color that matches the fabric
Embroidery thread DMC Cotton Perlé No. 8, in a matching color
Curved tapestry needle
Large mattress needle
Knitting needle
Four flat dressmaker buttons with shanks, in a color matching the main fabric
Metal thimble
Fine pins
Measuring stick
Tailor's chalk
Dressmaker's scissors

MEASUREMENTS

If you need to adapt the padded cushion so that it can be placed on the seat of an armchair or a spring mattress, measure the top of the desired shape (square or rectangular) as well as the thickness.

Nonetheless, the thickness should not exceed 8 inches if you are following the technique described here. The square cushion in the photograph opposite has a side of about 20 inches and is 6 inches thick.

FABRIC DIMENSIONS

The whole width of the fabric should be able to cover: The width of the cushion + the length of the bands + 2⅜ inches for seam allowances. Purchase enough fabric to cover the height measurement according to how thick you want your cushion to be.

CUTTING THE FABRIC

With damask, you can play with the "positive/negative" contrast of the two surfaces of the cloth.

On the wrong side of the fabric (the side where the white is the base color), trace two squares, each side 20 inches.

On the other side of the fabric (the side where the pink is the base color), trace four rectangles 20 inches by 6 inches.

Cut the pieces out ⅝ inch in from the trace mark.

On the right side of the pieces, trace a line ¾ inch from the edges while following the shape of the forms.

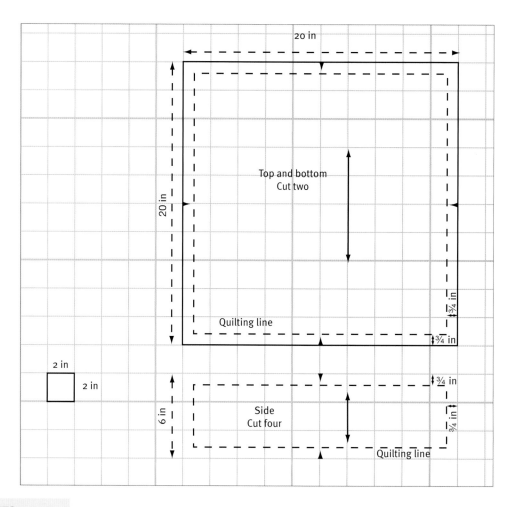

20 in

20 in

Top and bottom
Cut two

Quilting line

¾ in

¾ in

2 in

2 in

¾ in

6 in

Side
Cut four

¾ in

Quilting line

HELPFUL HINTS

When choosing ticking, give preference to a fabric with a locked weft, such as sailcloth or 100% cotton twill. These materials will be sturdier and will retain the stuffing in a more hermetic fashion. Such cushions, whether they are on some sort of support or not, tend to be more durable. Therefore you should choose quality materials to ensure the durability of the ensemble.

THE BACKSTITCH

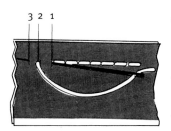

3 2 1

This stitch is used in Step 6 of the step-by-step photo of this project. It is worked from right to left on the right side of the fabric (see page 22 for an explanation of the technique).

For a project such as this, you will find it easier to work if you use a thimble for pushing the eye of the curved needle through the fabric.

THE PADDED CUSHION
IN 6 STEPS

Cut out the pieces from the ticking as previously indicated. Do not overcast the edges. For this model, you will not be doing any overcasting until after the assembly in Step 4.

1 JOINING THE SIDES TO THE TOP OF THE CUSHION

With the right sides of the fabric together, pin the four bands to the edges of the first square of fabric.

Stitch the pieces ⅝ inch from the edges, pivoting at corners (see page 73).

Press the seams open with an iron.

2 JOINING THE FOUR SIDE BANDS OF THE CUSHION

Stitch the widths of the bands of fabric to one another at each corner to form the box shape of the cushion.

3 JOINING THE BACK OF THE CUSHION

Matching corners, pin the second square of fabric on the assembled part.

Stitch ⅝ inch from the edge, leaving an opening of 10 inches in one of the sides.

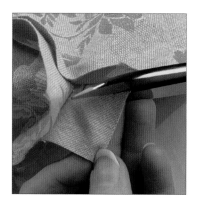

4 SEAM FINISHING

Press the seams open with an iron. Trim the corners and cut the seam allowances to ⅜ inch from the edge.

Carefully overcast the edges of the pieces with a zigzag stitch on the machine.

Turn the piece onto the right side.

5 STUFFING THE CUSHION

Slide the stuffing into the slipcover until the cushion is amply stuffed.

Tamp the stuffing down in the corners, using the knitting needle.

Close the opening by hand using a slipstitch.

6 QUILTING

Using the curved needle and Cotton Perle thread, stitch following the traced line on the top of the fabric. Use a small backstitch, making a tiny backstitch on the side surface, then a tiny backstitch of the top surface, followed by a longer stitch through the stuffing before the next backstitch on the side surface. These stitches will give shape to the quilting. Work all the edges of the squares and the corners in the same fashion.

FINISHING

Before you attach the buttons, mark their position with pins. Thread the mattress needle with a double strand of the Perle thread, and insert it into the back of the cushion.

Come through the entire thickness of the cushion, and attach the button on the front. Return needle and thread to cushion bottom. Tie the ends of the sting, pulling tightly, forming a relief pattern on the top of the work.

Making a Pleated Heading

PRELIMINARIES

Knowing how to make a pleated curtain heading is important and instructional. To succeed in this exercise, the first thing you need to do is to calculate precisely the width needed for a nice full curtain. By experimenting with the number and pattern of the pleats, you can achieve elegant and varied effects. The pleating method is also used on clothing when making skirts, blouses, and aprons, or for giving fullness to dresses.

MORE ABOUT THE TECHNIQUE

In general, when fashioning a curtain heading, the pleats are of equal width and are aligned side by side. The required fabric width for pleating is three times the width of the piece after pleating. There are different kinds of pleats: Flat pleats, knife pleats, round pleats, top-stitched round pleats, and box pleats. The construction of each of these is described here.

FLAT PLEATS

STEP 1

Mark even widths for the pleats with pins.

Form the pleats on the straight grain using an iron. Keep the pleats in place with a diagonal basting done across the top of the piece.

Machine stitch across the top of the pleating, ⅝ inch from the edge.

STEP 2

Now remove all the basting stitches.

When pressing, the bulk caused by the pleating may leave marks on the fabric. To avoid this, press the work with a sheet of tissue paper folded in four between each pleat.

KNIFE PLEATS

STEP 1

This step is the same as Step 1 for flat pleats.

STEP 2

Press the pleats as in Step 2 for flat pleats, but leaving basting in place.

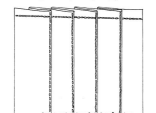

STEP 3

With pins, mark a line across pleats 1 or 2 inches below the top edge.

Stitch ¼ inch from the folded edge of each pleat from the top down to the marked line. Remove basting.

ROUND PLEATS

STEP 1

Mark even widths for the pleats with pins, allowing space between markers to accommodate this double-sided pleat.

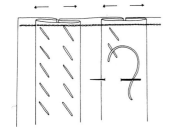

STEP 2

Fold half the pleat fullness to the left and half to the right, alternating pleated and plain surfaces. Press folds at the pleat edges and keep them in place with diagonal basting.

STEP 3

Topstitch pleats as in Step 3 of knife pleats.

STEP 4

Stitch across the top edge of fabrics ⅝ inch from the edge. Remove basting.

TOPSTITCHED ROUND PLEATS

STEP 1

Mark even widths for the pleats as in Step 1 for round pleats.

STEP 2

Fold, press, and baste pleats as in Step 2 for round pleats.

STEP 3

Topstitch pleats as in Step 3 of knife pleats.

STEP 4

Stitch across the top edge of fabrics ⅝ inch from the edge. Remove basting.

BOX PLEATS

STEP 1

The box pleat is simply an inverted round pleat, with the pleats formed at the back.

Prepare the fabric by flattening the round pleat to form a hollow between two pleats of the same width.

STEP 2

Keep the pleats in place with diagonal basting (see diagram).

Stitch along each side of the box pleat ¼ inch from the folded edge, making a few horizontal stitches across the base of the stitching to continue on the second edge.

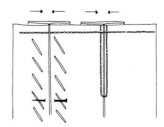

Stitch across the top edge ⅝ inch from the edge.

ON THE SEWING MACHINE

Having a good setting on the thread tension is the secret to obtaining a nice, even stitch and a good, clean seam.

Do a sample on a scrap of the cloth you are using or on a fabric equivalent in texture and thickness to it.

Verify the setting on your machine and place a thread of a contrasting color (to that of the bobbin) on the spool. That way you can better see which thread may need adjustment. Use a thread of the same weight in each.

Top Thread Tension

The stitch should be perfectly flat, without puckering the fabric. The bobbin thread will be passed through a thread guide mounted on an adjustable spring. If the top thread shows through on the other side of the fabric, then the tension is too slack, and so you need to increase it.

The thicker the thread, the higher the tension has to be for best results.

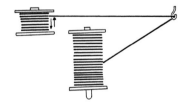

Bottom Thread Tension

On electric machines, the tension of this thread is regulated from the bobbin case. If the bobbin thread shows through on the top of the fabric, it is too slack. In this case, tighten the small screw in the bobbin case.

On newer electronic machines, the bottom thread tension is adjusted from the control panel where there is a graduated setting function (+ and −). This setting is not always easy to master, and sometimes it is necessary to revisit the top thread tension in order to perfect the setting.

The Double Curtain

The fullness of a double curtain makes it a good candidate for a heading consisting of voluminous pleats, called "round pleats." To do this type of work, you need a fabric that will hold its form, like cotton or thick linen, velvet, or even heavy cotton pique. If you would like to use a lighter fabric (like taffeta or a cotton blend), line the heading of the curtain with a stiffer fabric.

YOU WILL NEED

Striped taffeta, 63 inches wide (if necessary, join several whole fabric widths to get the desired width)
Lining, same measurements as the taffeta
Stiff interfacing, 1½ yards by 40 inches wide
Curtain hooks
Fine pins
Yardstick
Tailor's chalk
Dressmaker's scissors

HELPFUL HINTS

To help make the pleats, cut a piece of interfacing to the circumference of the pleat. Roll the piece up and slip it into the pleat to help maintain the shape.

MEASUREMENTS

In general, you would cut out both pieces of the double curtain at the same time.

The final width of each curtain corresponds to half the length of the curtain rod.

To obtain the length of the curtain, measure from the curtain rod all the way to the ground (or almost, if you prefer a shorter curtain).

FABRIC DIMENSIONS

Add 5½ inches per pleat to the final width of the curtain to obtain the exact width of fabric you will need.

The length of the fabric corresponds to the height measured from the curtain rod to the ground + 6 inches for the hems.

These are the measurements for a single curtain. Double these measurements to obtain the quantity of fabric needed to make of a pair of double curtains.

CUTTING THE FABRIC

On the striped taffeta, cut as many lengths of fabric as are necessary. Then, join the widths by stitching along the selvages ⅝ inch from the edges to get the full desired width of the curtain.

Carefully press the seams open with an iron.

Proceed in the same fashion with the fabric you have chosen for the lining.

THE DOUBLE CURTAIN IN 6 STEPS

The instructions given are for a single curtain. If you want to make a pair, simply repeat the instructions for the second panel. However if you introduce an asymmetrical detail, be sure to reproduce it exactly in mirror image on the second panel.

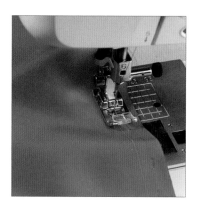

1 JOINING THE LINING

With the right side of the taffeta and lining facing, pin the two layers of fabric together at the top and about halfway down the sides. Stitch seams. Fold under the seam allowances on the lower half of the curtain along each side to form a small hem. Hand-sew the hems. Press the seams open and turn the piece right side out.

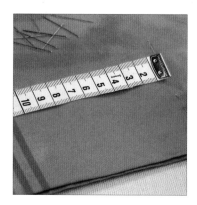

2 MARKING THE PLEATS

With the aid of pins, make 5½-inch-wide pleats at 5½-inch intervals along the top of the work.

Regardless of the procedure you choose, make the guide marks as even as you can if you want a neatly finished result.

3 MAKING ROUNDED PLEATS

Make the pleats by working on the wrong side of the fabric. Round out the emerging forms.

The pleats are situated on the front of the curtain. On the back of the work, carefully align the edges of the pleat markings, then pin.

SEWING THE PLEATS

Use your machine to sew 6 inches down from the top edge along each pleat working on the right side of the curtain.

Proceed slowly and carefully in order to avoid any mistakes.

MAKING ORGAN PIPE PLEATS

Another way to make rounded pleats is to pinch the curtain on the right side at the base of the pleat and then keep the pleat in place with a few back-stitches. You can also slip a piece of interfacing into the pleat (see the box on page 83).

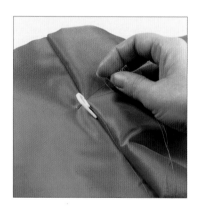

ATTACHING THE HOOKS

Sew on a hook 1½ inches from the top of the curtain, along the seam of the pleat, on the back of your work.

Also attach a hook on each end of the curtain so that it can be properly supported.

FINISHING

For the hems, use an iron to form a double fold of ¾ inch and 6 inches on the lining, and ¾ inch and 5⅛ inches on the taffeta. Sew the two hems separately. Using a slipstitch, sew by hand to finish the edges of the curtain and the lining.

Leave the bottom of the curtain as well as the bottom of the lining open; the lining should be ¾ inch shorter than the main fabric. Press the curtain, and attach it either to a wooden curtain rod or to a metal rail.

Making Gathers

PRELIMINARIES

Gathers can be found in numerous patterns: in the skirt of a dress, the flounce of a pillowcase, the ruffle of a bedspread, etc. Gathering is a simple technique with limitless applications.

Notwithstanding, it is important for you to give as much attention to the making of gathers as to the making of other finishes, since good work will enhance the overall effect of the piece, whether it be a garment or a decorative item.

MORE ABOUT THE TECHNIQUE

Making gathers requires the laying down of a basting stitch beforehand. Using thread of a contrasting color, baste the length of the piece to be gathered, then proceed in the order of the steps laid out opposite.

STEP 1

Gathers are sewn from right to left. Use a new, fine, short needle.

Beforehand, verify that the length of the thread in the needle is sufficient for covering up the entire surface to be gathered.

STEP 2

Support the fabric to be gathered in both hands. You should hold the needle between the thumb and index finger of your right hand (for a right-hander).

STEP 3

Moving your fists in opposite directions, slide the needle through using small running stitches.

Use a thimble to help you to push the eye of the needle through the fabric.

POINTS OF DETAIL

Not all fabrics can be gathered. Gathers work best on light or fine fabrics, but thick or heavy fabrics are difficult to put together if they are gathered. For these types of fabrics, it is better to use the pleating technique.

A DRESSMAKER'S TRICK

The assembly of a gathered piece and an straight (flat) one is done in the following manner: The gathered piece should be on top and the straight piece underneath, so that you can control the distribution of the folds along the entire length of the seam.

THE RUNNING STITCH

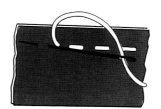

This stitch is commonly used for gathers. It is worked on the right side of the fabric, from right to left for the first row, then from left to right for the second row, and so on.

Use a new length of thread for each row and make the stitches small and as even as possible.

STEP 4

Make several stitches as indicated above, and then slide the gathered fabric along the length of thread.

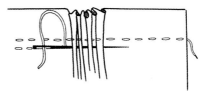

ON THE SEWING MACHINE

In order for the presser foot to be able to straddle the thickness of the gathers more easily during stitching, reduce the pressure of the presser foot a little.

Do a trial run beforehand on a scrap of fabric if you deem it necessary. Otherwise, begin sewing with care and proceed in stages, examining your work between each stage as you go along.

The Skirted Footrest

A classic footrest can take on quite another air when you outfit it with a very chic Scottish wool. This slipcover can also be done in other fabrics, such as striped taffetas, provincial prints, gingham, polka dots, and the like. Likewise, a round pouf can also be decked out in this kind of slipcover.

YOU WILL NEED

Woolen plaid, of a good quality, 1⅛ yards by 54 inches wide

Fine pins

Basting thread, in a color that contrasts against the main colors of the wool fabric

Basting needle

Plastic triangle

Yardstick

Tailor's chalk

Dressmaker's scissors

MEASUREMENTS

Measure the top of the footrest that you would like to cover with a slipcover.

Measure the height from the top of the bare pouf to the ground.

FABRIC DIMENSIONS

Verify that you can get the band for the gathered ring from the width of the fabric.

If the width is insufficient, cut the number of bands necessary for making the ring and join these bands with a plain seam, matching fabric stripes.

The rectangle forming the top of the footrest should correspond to the dimensions of the pad + 1½ inches extra all around for the seams.

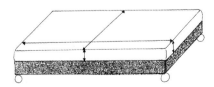

HELPFUL HINTS

To get a nice fullness when gathering, double the perimeter of the object, the piece of occasional furniture, or the article of clothing that you want to finish with a ruffle.

CUTTING THE FABRIC

Using the tailor's chalk, mark out on the right side of the fabric the rectangle for the top of the footrest as well as the band (including the side edges joined to the ruffle) for the ring.

Cut the pieces out ⅜ inch from the trace mark.

Cut the four corners of the top piece ⅜ inch from the trace mark (see the pattern below).

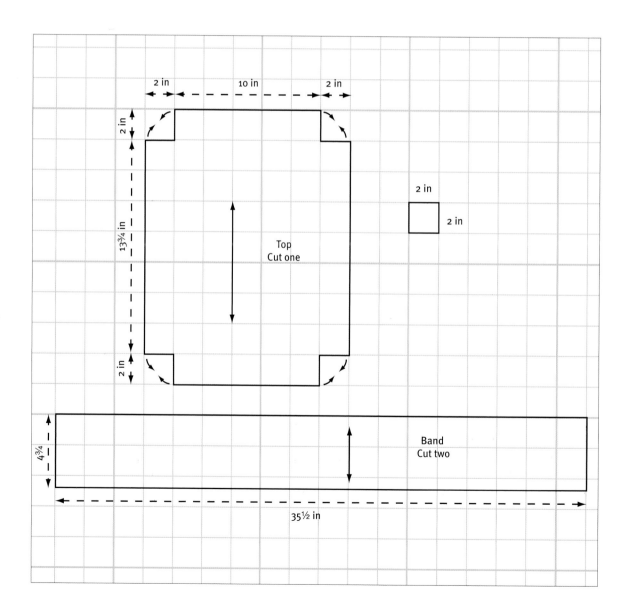

2 in   10 in   2 in

2 in

13¾ in

2 in

Top
Cut one

2 in

2 in

2 in

4¾

Band
Cut two

35½ in

THE STRAIGHT STITCH

This machine stitch is used in Step 2 (as illustrated in the photo) of the step-by-step guide for this pattern. It allows you to join together several total fabric widths to obtain the fabric width you desire.

Make sure to keep the piece flat as you work, to prevent the fabric from puckering. Adjust the thread tension according to the material (see page 82). Begin and end the stitch with a few stitches made by going backward, and cut the thread as close to the seam as possible.

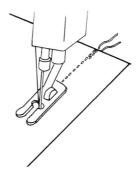

THE SKIRTED FOOTREST IN 4 STEPS

Before proceeding with the steps below, overcast the pieces. Remember: The more care you take in doing the gathers (basting, stitching, gathering, assembly), the better your final product will be.

1 MAKING THE CORNERS OF THE TOP PIECE

With the right sides of the fabric together, fold the four corners that you previously cut in the top piece of the footrest, and pin.

Stitch and trim each corner back to be able to open the seams completely by pressing.

HEMING THE SKIRT RUFFLE

Join the ruffle bands end to end to make a long strip, using a straight stitch. With an iron, press a fold of ⅜ inch along one edge; pin in place. Press a second fold of ⅝ inch. Baste the hem with a straight stitch ⅜ inch from the edge.

MAKING THE GATHERS

Thread a needle with a piece of thread that is the length of the finished ring + 6 inches. With small, even stitches, make the first gather line. Using another length of thread, make a second line ⅜ inch from the first. Spread the gathers out evenly along the length of the ring by pulling on the threads. The length should be equal to the perimeter of the seat + ¾ inch for seam allowances.

Tie the gather threads together at each end, to keep the desired length of the ring.

JOINING THE RING TO THE TOP PIECE

With the right sides facing, pin the two ends of the gathered ring together and stitch the ring along its height.

With the right sides together, place the gathered ring over the top piece, matching the gathered ring edge to the edges of the top. Baste, spreading the gathers out evenly. Stitch ⅝ inch from the edge, with the gathered ring over the top and the flat top piece against the feed dogs.

FINISHING

Press to turn down the seam allowances of your work toward the flat part of the slipcover. Place the slipcover on the footrest.

For a crisper finish, hand-sew a flat braid on so that it straddles the assembly seam.

Smocking

PRELIMINARIES

Smocking is more closely related to embroidery than to sewing. This play of reembroidered pleats can be used to embellish certain parts of a garment. They can be found on baby chemises, on the bodice of dresses for small girls, on the yokes of blouses for women, and on lingerie. Today, with the improvements to sewing machines, smocking has become quick and easy.

MORE ABOUT THE TECHNIQUE

Smocking needs to be done before the assembly step. First of all, you need to gather the fabric along the width and height indicated on the pattern. Next is the embroidery step, which you can do by hand or, as indicated here, by machine (electronic machines offer a wide selection of embroidered edges).

STEP 1

Cut your piece of fabric, taking into account that the width required will be four times the final width of the smocking. If the fabric is not checkered, attach a squared zephyr cloth to the back of it (see the box and the text on page 97); it can serve as a guide.

On this cloth, trace out a rectangle of the width of the fabric to be gathered and of the desired height of the smocking. Cut out 1⅜ inches from the trace line. Overcast the edges, and using an iron, apply the zephyr cloth to the wrong side of the other fabric.

STEP 2

Thread a needle with a length of thread equivalent to the width of the fabric to be gathered + 6 inches. Make a secure knot at the end of the thread.

Work a row of gathers, progressing from right to left. Use the squares in the fabric or on the zephyr cloth to guide you in making even, regular stitches.

When you reach the end of a row, do not cut the thread; rather, leave it hanging in anticipation of being tied off later.

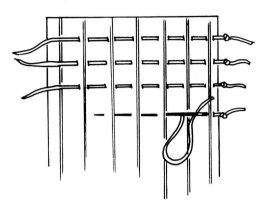

STEP 3

Once the gather threads have been sewn into the fabric, verify that all the surface stitches are aligned one on top of the other, at equal intervals.

Lay your piece of fabric flat and gently pull on the threads one by one until you achieve the width you prefer.

The pleats formed should be very even. Should a gather thread break, lay the cloth flat and pass a new thread through the row that was undone.

STEP 4

When you have pulled all the threads, tie off the ends of the free thread of each row two by two in order to keep the gathers in place.

STEP 5

Adjust the sewing machine to the embroidery design of your choice. Load it with a special machine embroidering thread (size 30 or 40) in a matching or a contrasting color.

Install the presser foot recommended by the manufacturer for this type of work and embroider a few rows of the shirring.

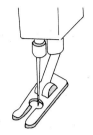

THE PRESSER FOOT

The presser foot is also called a sewing foot. There are feet other than the sewing foot that can be bought separately.

Certain embroidery stitches require the installation of a particular presser foot.

Follow the instructions provided by the retailer or in the manual that came with your machine. Also see the descriptions and diagrams of the different presser feet, page 21.

STEP 6

When you have finished embroidering, gently pull out all the gather threads — except the ones at the top and bottom of the yoke (or the area of the smocking).

ON THE SEWING MACHINE

Many domestic sewing machine models offer novelty stitches.

For the pattern that follows, we have chosen a simple stitch, the feather stitch. Set the machine to this stitch and install the appropriate presser foot.

Use a special machine embroidering thread (size 30 to 40) in a color that matches the fabric. Fill a spool with this same thread.

Release the pressure of the presser foot a little in order to be able to work the stitch. Guide the pleats straight under the presser foot to keep them from flattening out. Smocking done on the machine is barely distinguishable from smocking done by hand.

The Child's Dress

The sun dress is the simplest dress to make. However, making a bodice of smocking still requires time and precision. The model presented here is for a 4-year-old girl; but since the pattern is made of rectangles, all you have to do to adapt the pattern to another size is to measure the height and bust of the child for whom the dress is intended.

YOU WILL NEED

Fine cotton, with small checks, two dress lengths
Drapery thread, in a color matching the base color of the fabric
Special machine embroidery thread size 40, in a contrasting color
Long sewing needle
Fine pins
Yardstick
Dressmaker's scissors

HELPFUL HINTS

It is useful to work on a checkered fabric because the checks serve as a guide for making the gathers. If the cloth you are using is not checkered, it is advisable to affix a piece of zephyr cloth to the back of your working fabric.

MEASUREMENTS

For the width of the dress, take the chest measurement of the child as shown on page 247.

For the dress length, measure the height from the shoulder to the ground.

FABRIC DIMENSIONS

The width of the fabric should be four times the child's chest measurement + 2 inches for the seams.

The length of the fabric is equal to twice the height measurement you obtained above (for the front and the back pieces of the dress).

ZEPHYR CLOTH

This supple cotton textile is imprinted with a fine grid that makes it easier to sew in gather threads so that you will not need to use chalk markings.

If you cannot find zephyr fabric, you can use transfer paper that has dotted lines printed on it instead. These sheets are sold by the envelope in the same stores where you can buy patterns.

Pin the paper to the back of the fabric. Pass the sole of a warm iron over the paper; let it cool, then remove the paper. The dots will be transferred to the back of the fabric.

CUTTING THE FABRIC

Line up the pattern along the straight grain and transfer the rectangles for the front and the back of the dress onto the wrong side of the checkered fabric. Then mark out the length of the yoke.

Also, trace out the small rectangles for the shoulder straps for the dress.

Child's dress, age 4

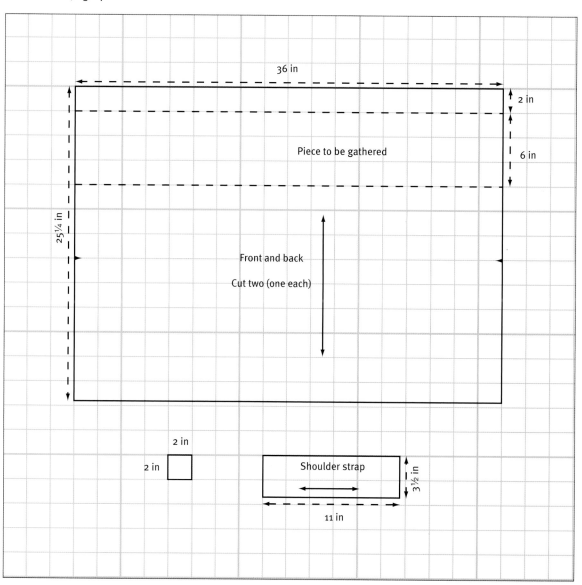

THE CHILD'S DRESS IN 5 STEPS

Determine ahead of time what design you would like to have on the yoke. When smocking, do not use motifs that are too small because even though they might be cute, they have the tendency to tamp down the pleats.

1 PREPARING THE GATHERS

At the top of each large rectangle, form a double hem of 1⅜ inches with an iron. Use a running stitch to sew it down. Begin working the gathers 2 inches from the top and 1³⁄₁₆ inches from the sides of the first rectangle.

Stitch along one horizontal line of the fabric design, then skip two lines of the motif (or about ⅝ inch) before starting the row.

Proceed in the same manner for the second rectangle of fabric.

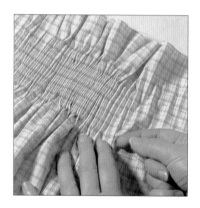

2 MAKING PLEATS FOR EMBROIDERING

Once you have finished stitching, lay the fabric flat on a table.

Pull the gather threads one by one until you have obtained the smock width you desire.

Set the widths of the gather threads with a small knot and tie off the floating threads two by two to keep it all together.

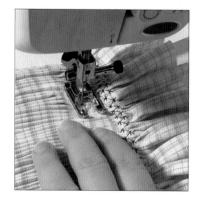

3 EMBROIDERING THE YOKE

Set the gathered yoke under the presser foot of the sewing machine. Embroider the first row of the design ¾ inch from the top of the gathered area.

Sew, following the horizontal line of the checkered motif to keep embroidered design quite straight.

Next, repeat this operation several times to cover the width of the yoke at even intervals.

ASSEMBLING THE FRONT AND BACK PIECES OF THE DRESS

4 Recut the sides of the front and back rectangles of the dress, removing ⅝ inch of fabric from each end. Carefully overcast the edges.

With the right sides of the fabric facing, pin the now even sides of these rectangles together and stitch, taking care not to let the fabric shift.

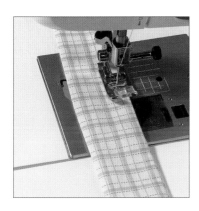

ATTACHING THE STRAPS

5 Fold the rectangles for the shoulder straps in half lengthwise, wrong side facing in, then assemble using a French seam (see "More About the Technique," page 42).

Press the seams flat with an iron. Fold the ends ⅝ inch toward the interior of the straps, and stitch closed. Try the dress on the child. Position the straps to the desired length, pin them together, then stitch.

FINISHING

Using the iron, make a first fold of ⅝ inch in the bottom of the dress and baste.

Make another fold of 2 inches on the first, adjusting the height of the hem to the height of the child.

Pin the folds and stitch ⅜ inch above the hemline.

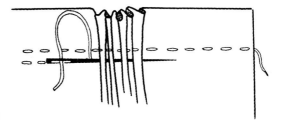

Preparing gathers

Attaching a Collar

PRELIMINARIES

In clothing construction, attaching a collar is an important step. Collars come in numerous forms: flat collar, notched collar, tailored collar, mandarin collar, sailor collar, shawl collar, Peter Pan collar, shirt collar, Mao collar, etc.

In general, a collar is composed of three layers: a top piece, a bottom piece, and interfacing. The pattern may present two different pieces for the top collar and the bottom collar; in this case the first piece would be a little bigger than the second.

MORE ABOUT THE TECHNIQUE

Transfer the outlines to the wrong side of the fabric. Trace the piece for the bottom collar on both the main fabric and the interfacing at the same time. Do not forget to copy the assembly marks indicated on the pattern before cutting out the pieces.

STEP 1

Attach the iron-on interfacing to the wrong side of the piece for the bottom collar (see "Interfacing," page 16).

Very carefully press it on with an iron.

STEP 2

With the right sides facing, stitch around the edge of the collar with the interfaced collar bottom piece against the feed of the sewing machine. Do this in two steps: Begin working from the center back of the collar, and stitch first one part, then the other, from this middle point. Leave the collar bottom open.

STEP 3

Trim the seam allowances a scant ³⁄₁₆ inch from the edges.

Free up the points of the collar by trimming off the excess fabric around the corners.

STEP 4

Press the seam open with an iron.

Turn the seam allowances under toward the bottom collar piece.

STEP 5

Open the collar as if it were a pocket.

On the right side of the fabric and on the top collar piece, stitch as close as possible to the assembly seam.

STEP 6

Turn the collar onto the right side, using a pin to turn out the points. First press the surface of the collar bottom and finish off by pressing the collar top.

Roll the seam toward the collar bottom piece.

STEP 7

Even up the edges that were left open and baste with a long slanted stitch on the same side as the outer stitching.

This basting will be removed once the collar is permanently attached.

STEP 8

With the right sides together, baste the bottom of the collar onto the neckline while paying attention to the assembly markings.

STEP 9

Stitch the inside of the collar to the neckline, with the facing directed toward you. Cut the seam allowances, and use an iron to press them flat toward the inside of the collar.

STEP 10

Using the iron, turn the fold of the collar top toward the inside. Use a slipstitch to close the collar.

ON THE SEWING MACHINE

To make the outer seam of the collar, adjust the length of the stitch: scant ⅛ inch on the straight lines and 1/16 inch for the points.

In the corners, accurately make a diagonal stitch at the point.

Attaching a Cuff

PRELIMINARIES

Cuffs can be used to finish a piece, and can be applied to various parts of a garment: to the bottoms of the legs of pants or shorts; to the ends of the long, short, or three-quarter sleeves of a dress; to a jacket; or, as in the model in the photograph on page 107, to the sleeves of a blouse.

It is also possible to mount a cuff on a pocket.

Regardless of the application, however, the general technique remains the same.

MORE ABOUT THE TECHNIQUE

The mounting of a cuff on a leg or a sleeve is similar to that for a collar, with respect to the transfer of the pattern to the fabric, the markings, and the general finishing principles. However the form of the pieces and the assembly phases are inevitably different. The instructions show the preparation of the pieces of the cuff onward.

STEP 1

On the pattern for the bottom of the sleeve, add a band whose length corresponds to twice the length of the cuff + 1³⁄₁₆ inches for the hem.

Trace out three parallel lines: The first is the lower fold line of the cuff, the second is the hem edge of the cuff, and the third is the cutting line of the cuff.

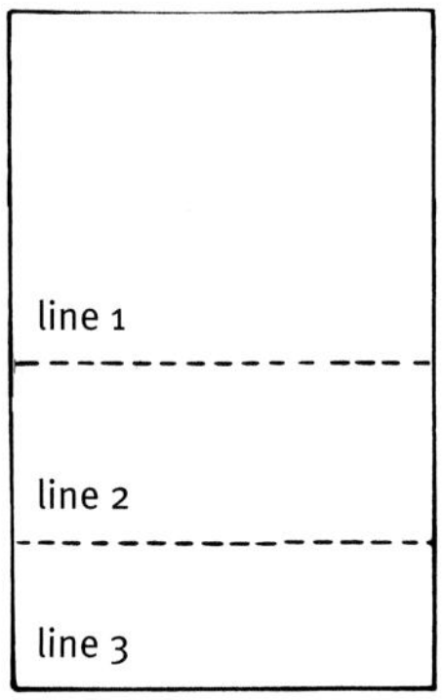

line 1
line 2
line 3

STEP 2

Fold the paper of the pattern as follows, in order to obtain the final length of the finished cuff.

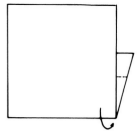

Cut the side of the cuff a little wider than the width of the sleeve. Unfold the band of the cuff and trace your pattern on the back of the fabric. Cut out the pieces. Mark and baste the three fold lines.

STEP 3

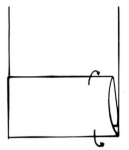

Stitch the underarm seam of sleeves, clipping allowance, then reversing seam below line 1 to prevent seam edges from showing when cuff is turned up. Sew sleeves to armholes. Press seams open. Turn up the cuff along line 1.

STEP 4

Baste or pin the cuff thus formed. Make a fold of 1³⁄₁₆ inches with an iron in preparation for hemming (line 2).

Pin the length of this fold and stitch ⅜ inch from the edge through cuff layers, omitting sleeve layer.

STEP 5

On the right side, refold cuff along the lower edge (line 1). Pin and baste through all layers, then press the fold.

STEP 6

Along the vertical sleeve seam, tack the cuff in place, and tack the inner layers discreetly on the opposite side of the sleeve.

ON THE SEWING MACHINE

It is absolutely necessary that you make the stitches of the sleeve assembly (see Step 3 above) reversed so that they will be completely covered when the cuff is folded back.

The Blouse

In this blouse project we see the application of the two techniques that were just presented, the construction of collars and the assembly of cuffs. These two techniques are popularly used in garment construction and do not vary much from one type of garment to another. In fact, while the shape of the collar may vary, the process of assembling one does not. Cuffs, whether they are situated at the bottom of a pant leg, at the sleeve ends of a jacket, or the edge of a pocket, are all made the same way.

YOU WILL NEED

Checkered gingham, 2 yards by 44 inches wide
Lightweight interfacing, ¾ yard by 24 inches
Sewing thread, in white
Fine pins
Six decorative snap fasteners
Tailor's chalk
Dressmaker's scissors

HELPFUL HINTS

To ease in the excess of the sleeve during assembly (see Step 8 of the step-by-step procedure), stretch out the curved part of the armhole by gently pulling on the fabric; this should reduce the fullness somewhat.

MEASUREMENTS
Take the bust measurement and the front shoulder to waist length. Also measure the back waist length.

   Check that the pattern fits these measurements; make any necessary adjustments.

FABRIC DIMENSIONS
For sizes 12 to 16: 2 yards of fabric 44 inches in width, or 1¼ yards of fabric at least 55 inches in width.

THE INTERFACING
Interfacing is used in this project to line the collar and the fronts of the blouse.

size 14 blouse

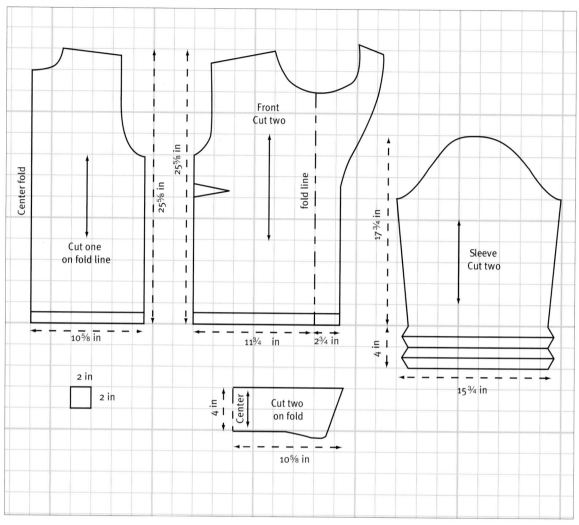

CUTTING THE FABRIC

Seam allowances are included in the pattern above: 1 inch for the bottom hem allowances and ⅝ inch for the seam allowances.

Fold the fabric in half, right sides together. Pin the two layers together. Position the center of the back pattern piece over the fabric fold line. Trace the outlines of the pattern onto the fabric using a piece of tailor's chalk. Cut out this part of the piece and transfer the assembly markings onto the other side of the back.

Lay the pattern pieces for the fronts, the sleeves and the collar onto the double layer of fabric. Trace their outlines using the chalk then cut them out along the lines. Carefully transfer the assembly marks onto each of the fabric pieces.

Cut the collar and blouse front facings from the interfacing.

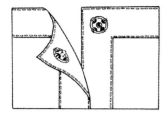

SNAP AND HOOK-AND-EYE FASTENERS

A **snap fastener** consists of two round pieces that snap and fit together. The perimeter of each piece should have three or four holes which allow it to be sewn onto an item. Snap fasteners come in a variety of sizes; choose one according to the item and the nature of the fabric you are working with.

Use pins to mark the attachment points for the pieces of the snap fasteners. First sew the piece that has the stud and stitch three or four times through each of the holes that edge it. This piece should be attached to the wrong side of the button flap.

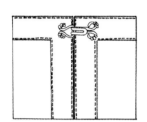

Apply chalk to the piece that you have just sewn on and press it against the part of the item where the other piece of the fastener should be situated. Sew the other fastener piece onto the area marked by the chalk. For decorative or riveted snap fasteners that have four pieces, follow the instructions given by the manufacturer.

The **hook-and-eye fastener** may come in plain metal or in metal covered by braiding or trimming, and consists of two pieces: a flat or curved loop and a hook. Attach the curved parts of each piece by hand.

THE BLOUSE IN 8 STEPS

Overcast the pattern pieces before you begin assembly. Create the bust darts and stitch them first. Lay the two fronts onto the back, right sides together. Pin them together then sew along the shoulders. Press the seams open with an iron.

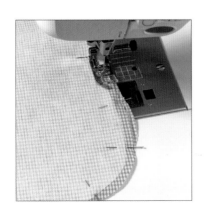

1 PREPARING FRONTS FOR THE COLLAR FACING

Pin the pieces of interfacing onto the wrong side of the two blouse fronts.

Using a long zigzag stitch, attach the blouse fronts onto the outside edge of the interfacing (see the technique for assembling two pieces with a zigzag stitch on page 25).

2 PREPARING THE FRONT FACINGS

Fold the two front interfacings along the assembly markings, right sides together. Pin them together along these markings. You will assemble these pieces after you have completed the collar which is described in Step 4, below.

3 PREPARING THE COLLAR

Lay the collar interfacing onto the wrong side of one collar piece (collar bottom). Pin them together, then join with a large zigzag stitch around the edge. With right sides together, lay the top collar over the interfaced back. Pin, then stitch along the outer edges. Trim the seam allowances to ¼ inch from the seam and trim corners. Press the seams open. Turn the collar right side out. Press and carefully topstitch around the outer edge.

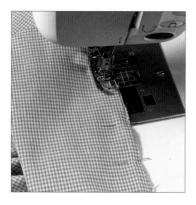

4 COMPLETING THE COLLAR

Open the collar like a pocket. Align the center of the bottom collar to the center of the back neckline; pin these edges together along the neckline. Clip the seam allowance of the front collar at each shoulder seam and pin each end of the front collar seam to ends of the back collar. Turn the front interfacings back over the collar edge and press. Lifting the front collar edge between clips out of the way, baste and stitch the collar seam, catching the top edge of the facing in the seam. Omitting the unsewn section of the front collar, notch the collar seam allowances.

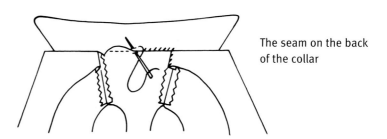

The seam on the back of the collar

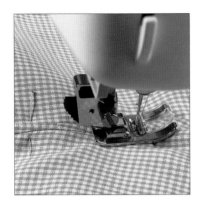

5 TOPSTITCHING THE BASE OF THE COLLAR

Fold under the remaining edge of the front collar. Pressing the collar seam just made into the collar, press the front fold. With a slip stitch, sew the upper edges of the facing to the shoulder seams and close the front collar (see the diagram on the opposite page).

Topstitch the base of the collar as evenly as you can ⅛ inch from the seam that you just made. The care that you put into completing these two seams will determine how neat the finish of the collar will be.

6 SEWING THE ARMHOLES

Lay the two blouse fronts over the back fabric piece. Baste, then seam the sides. Press the seams open with an iron.

Reinforce the heads of the sleeves with two rows of stitching by machine, ¼ inch from the edge. You will join the sleeves to the armholes in Step 8.

7 CONSTRUCTING THE SLEEVE CUFFS

Fold the sleeves in two, lengthwise. Pin the sides together, reversing the seam at folds so the raw edges are not exposed when the cuff is turned up. Stitch. Press the seams open with an iron.

Continue using the iron to fold the sleeve cuffs in the direction indicated on the pattern. Pin them together, then baste.

Keep the cuffs in place by a stitch done by hand in the bottom seam and on the top of each sleeve.

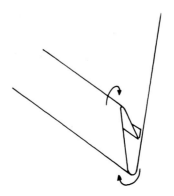

The final cuff fold

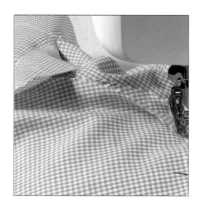

8 JOINING THE SLEEVES TO THE ARMHOLES

Pin the sleeves onto the armholes, right sides together, while paying attention to the pattern markings.

Spread the excess fabric out evenly to avoid the formation of folds along the curves.

Pin, baste, then stitch, starting from the bottom of the sleeves. Notch the seam reserves and fold them back with an iron in the same direction as the sleeves rather than that of the body of the blouse.

FINISHING

Use an iron to fold the hem allowances to the wrong side. Turn under a first fold that is ¼ inch in width, then turn a second fold over the first, ⅝ inch wide. Pin them in place.

Turn the bottom of the facings onto the hem. Baste, then stitch. Use a piece of tailor's chalk to mark the six sites where the snap fasteners will go along both edges of the blouse.

Apply the decorative snap fasteners by following the manufacturer's instructions. Also refer to the explanations on page 109.

If you have difficulty finding suitable decorative snap fasteners, you can use regular snap fasteners, sewn to the overlapping front edges, then sew a button to the outer front at each snap position. The buttons are purely decorative.

Or, you can try your hand at making real buttonholes, following the directions beginning on page 169.

4

LININGS

Making Cases

PRELIMINARIES

Linings can give an elegant finish to an item. Sometimes they are very simple, as in the case of a pillowcase, or more complex, as in the kimono and the jacket that are presented later in this chapter. Beyond their aesthetic quality, linings may offer other benefits: They may add warmth as in the case of a padded lining; or they may afford comfort as in the lining of a pair of pants or a skirt constructed from fabrics that are somewhat rough.

MORE ABOUT THE TECHNIQUE

Cases can be used with bed linen as well as with decorative cushions. A pillowcase is usually made from durable, smooth fabrics that are 100% linen or 100% cotton. Cotton percale, cotton velvet and various varieties of silk are used for covering cushions.

STEP 1

On the wrong side of the fabric, trace the outlines of a piece that corresponds to the dimensions of the cushion or the pillowcase. Cut the piece out ⅜ inch beyond the traced lines to allow for seams.

For the two back pieces, trace an outline that measures the width of the cushion by the total of half the length + 6 inches extra. Cut these pieces out ⅜ inch beyond the traced lines.

STEP 2

Complete a ⅜-inch hem along the lower edge of the two back fabric pieces that you just cut out.

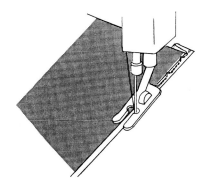

STEP 3

With the right sides together, place the two back pieces on top of the front piece, overlapping the hemmed edges at the center. Stitch the side ⅜ inch from the outer edges.

STEP 4

Trim the corners and press the seams open with an iron. Turn the case right side out.

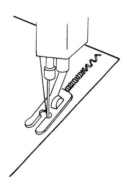

ON THE SEWING MACHINE

The satin stitch, which is often used to edge pillowcases, can be completed on any sewing machine that is capable of executing a zigzag stitch.

If you have a special satin stitch foot, install it onto your sewing machine. This foot is unique in that it has a hollowed sole that lets the raised stitch pass through. Set the stitch length to 1/16 inch and the stitch width to ⅛ inch at a minimum. On certain machines, it is possible to widen the stitch to 3/16 inch.

Try out the technique on a small scrap of fabric from the work in progress to verify that the stitch tension for the bobbin threads is correct (see the guidelines on page 82).

The Pillowcase

The pillowcase is a classic mainstay where bed linen is concerned. This is one of the most practically shaped cases there is and the easiest one to make. The top and bottom pieces can be joined in no time. The fabric that is used here is not only smooth and durable, but makes the project a whole lot easier to complete. The shape used to make this case is also used for decorative cushions.

YOU WILL NEED

Linen or cotton fabric, 1⅛ yards by 60 inches wide (for a square case measuring 28½ inches on a side)

Sewing thread, in a color that matches the main fabric

Special machine embroidery thread, size 40, in a contrasting color

Fine pins

Plastic triangle

Yardstick

Tailor's chalk

HELPFUL HINTS

The overlapped edges on the back of the case should be deep enough to keep the pillow in its case. Before you start, make sure you allow for a large enough length of fabric and take any required excess into consideration when you start cutting out the fabric pieces.

MEASUREMENTS

Begin by taking the measurements for your pillow, regardless of whether it is of a standard size or not. Then decide on what finishing you would like to apply to the case.

Here, a flat border accented with a satin stitch worked in an embroidery thread of a contrasting color all around its edge, gives the pillowcase an original touch.

FABRIC DIMENSIONS

For a square case measuring 24 inches per side, you will need a piece of fabric measuring 1⅛ yards by 60 inches in width. You can adjust these dimensions to suit the shape of your pillow.

For a flat border that is 1⅝ inches in width, add 3⅛ inches to the length and the width of the fabric, ¾ inch of which is for the fullness of the pillow itself.

CUTTING THE FABRIC

On the wrong side of the fabric, outline a square measuring 24 inches per side, a rectangle measuring 24 inches by 16 inches and another rectangle measuring 24 inches by 10 inches. Cut the fabric pieces out ¾ inch from the trace marks.

On the top of the square, outline a second square whose sides are 2 inches from the edge of the first; 1⅝ inches of the width is for the border and ⅜ inch is for the seam allowance. This inner square is not for cutting; you will use it as a reference point when making the border.

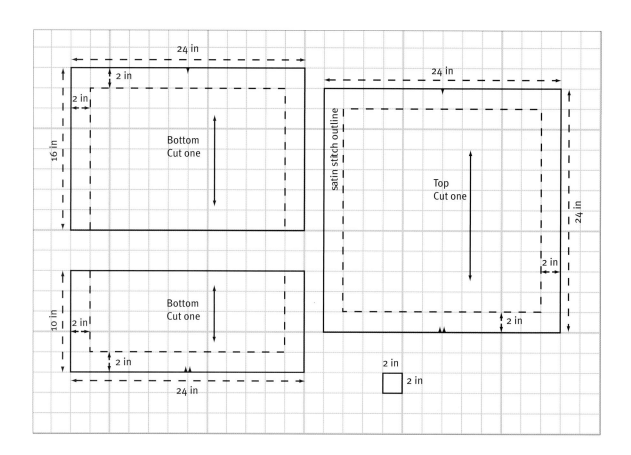

THE PILLOWCASE IN 4 STEPS

After you have overcast the three pieces of fabric that will be used to construct the pillowcase, the square, and the two rectangles, carry out the following steps.

1 COMPLETING THE HEMS OF THE PILLOWCASE

Use an iron to first make one fold then a second over it so that you create a ⅜-inch hem along the lower edge of each of the bottom pieces of the pillowcase. Stitch these two hems on the sewing machine, but take care that the fabric does not pucker.

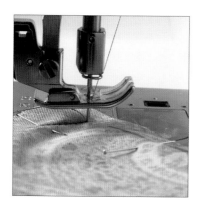

JOINING THE FABRIC PIECES

With the right sides together, pin the two bottom fabric pieces on top of the top fabric piece, overlapping the hemmed edges.

Set the smaller rectangle in place last; once you turn the case inside out, it should be beneath the larger rectangle, forming the back of the case.

Stitch the sides within ¾ inch of the edge. Trim the corners.

PREPARING FOR THE SATIN STITCH

Carefully press the seams open with an iron and turn the pillowcase out onto its right side out.

Stitch along the top of the case by following the outline of the inner square while holding all three layers of fabric together.

MAKING THE SATIN STITCH

Load the embroidery thread onto the bobbin pins and use the satin stitch foot on the sewing machine if you have one.

Adjust the machine for a zigzag stitch with a width of at least ⅛ inch and a length of at least ¹⁄₁₆ inch. Work the satin stitch over the seam that delineates the inner square of the case.

FINISHING

Press the pillowcase, paying special attention to the flat borders, but make sure that you do not flatten the satin stitch.

While the body of the case is the centerpiece of this item, it is the border that adds the appeal. Devote an adequate amount of time toward its completion.

The Reversible Lining

PRELIMINARIES

This kind of lining is especially suited to garments that are not faced and whose shape is relatively simple.

The lining is attached edge to edge to the right side of the garment and in this way should entirely cover the interior of the piece. This is why it is possible to reverse the piece for use, as in the case of the kimono that is presented later.

MORE ABOUT THE TECHNIQUE

The reversible lining offers several advantages. It makes up for the absence of facings, protects the main fabric, conceals any internal seams, makes it easier to put on and take off the garment and, most importantly, gives you the choice of wearing it on the wrong or the right side.

STEP 1

Assemble the top of the garment along the shoulder seams. Attach the sleeves to the armhole edges.

Always work with the right sides of the fabric against each other. Seam the side and sleeve seams.

STEP 2

Assemble the fabric pieces of the lining in the same way that you did for the garment itself.

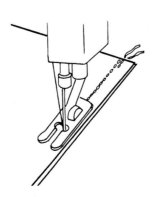

POINTS OF DETAIL

Carefully baste all the fabric pieces to prevent them from slipping over each other when you start working. The lining should be cut from a fabric that is not the main fabric; the lining material should be finer, silkier, and more slippery.

A DRESSMAKER'S TRICK

On fuller garments, the last step (Step 5) may be replaced by the construction of a hem in the main fabric and a second hem a little bit higher, more than ⅜ inch, in the lining; it will keep the two faces of the garment separate. This technique allows you to avoid creasing later on. This is what is called a free-hanging lining (see the adjacent diagram).

STEP 3

With right sides together, place the lining over the garment, lining up corresponding shoulder, side, and sleeve seams. Pin and baste edges together along front edges and neckline. Stitch ⅜ inch from edges. Press seams open.

STEP 4

Turn the garment right side out through the bottom edge, with lining sleeves inside the garment sleeves. At the ends of the sleeves, fold in ⅜ inch of lining and of garment so raw seam edges fall between lining and outer garment; press the folds. By hand, slipstitch the folded edge of the lining to the garment around each sleeve edge.

STEP 5

Use an iron to create inward folds along both the main fabric and the lining. Avoid forming creases and make sure that the lining does not end up obstructing the fullness of the garment.

Close off the bottom hem of the garment using a slipstitch unless you are opting for a free-hanging lining (see the "Dressmaker's Trick" sidebar).

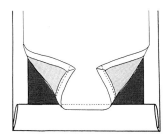

ON THE SEWING MACHINE

When stitching the lining onto the garment, let the lining face toward you.

You should do this because the lining is usually made from a material that is finer than the main fabric of the garment and it could get caught on the feed dogs of the sewing machine.

A Lesson on Hems

PRELIMINARIES

A hem is made using either a single or a double fold. Hems make it possible to finish the edges of an item that are not concealed by seams; they draw a piece together while creating a more aesthetically pleasing result. In certain cases, a hem also makes it possible for you to hang onto excess fabric in the event of future modifications.

MORE ABOUT THE TECHNIQUE

Before you make a hem, it is very important to mark the hemline. There are several ways to do this: pins or basting thread, a fold created by an iron, or a trace line created using a hem gauge. All three of these methods require the use of a yardstick. This section presents some of the most popular techniques for making a hem and are used with garments as well as with decorative items.

THE BASTING METHOD

STEP 1

Calculate and mark the desired height of the bottom hemline. Baste along this hemline.

STEP 2

Fold the hem to the wrong side along the basted line. Pin, then baste layers together ⅜ inch above the folded hemline.

STEP 3

Check that the hemline is correct; fix any imbalances. When the hemline is satisfactory, trim the top edge to make the depth of the hem even from the fold line. Fold under ⅝ inch along the top of the hem. Baste all three layers together ⅜ inch below the top fold line.

The pressing technique presented here is quick and useful. However, avoid pressing fragile fabrics that are easily "marked." In the case of a mistake, gently flatten out the fabric with an iron, then take up the process again with as much precision as you can.

A DRESSMAKER'S TRICK

Sometimes it can be very useful to be able to extend or lengthen a hem on a garment or a lined curtain. To provide for this possibility, allow for an extra length of fabric equal to ¼ inch less than the length of the current hem. When you want to extend the hem, first undo it and then smooth out the interior. Then either shape a false hem or complete a bound hem using a piece of binding tape (see page 124). If the former hem has left an outline, press it out using a pressing cloth that has been soaked with spirit vinegar.

THE PRESSING METHOD

STEP 1

Use an iron to fold the fabric so that the wrong sides are together, while paying attention to any measurements that you have taken. Place a pressing cloth between the fabric and the sole of the iron. Work from the outer edge toward the interior of the hem, easing any excess fullness. Then let the hem cool down and dry.

STEP 2

If the piece is lined, fold the fabric while creating a second hem fold that is higher than the first. Lightly press the edge of the hem using the tip of the iron while working from the outer edge toward the interior of the hem.

To keep the first hem fold from leaving an impression on the right side of the material, place a sheet of brown wrapping paper between the hem and the wrong side of the fabric.

THE HEM GAUGE METHOD

STEP 1

Cut out an 8- by 6-inch rectangle from a piece of Bristol board of medium thickness and trace out parallel lines on it that correspond to the hem heights.

STEP 2

Place the gauge against the wrong side of the fabric and fold the edge of the fabric to the desired height. Use an iron to flatten the fold; be sure to place a pressing cloth between the fabric and the sole of the iron. Work by sliding the iron from the outer edge toward the interior of the hem.

ON THE SEWING MACHINE

Manufacturers usually offer a hemmer foot, which allows you to create and stitch the hem in one step. Limit the use of this foot to thin fabrics such as cotton blends.

THE BASIC TURNED-UP HEM

This is a simple hem that is used as a finishing on flat items. It consists of a single fold and should not be especially difficult to make.

THE HERRINGBONE STITCHED HEM

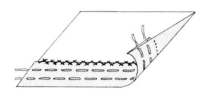

This hem is especially suitable for thick fabrics like wool, but it can be used in other cases as well. Usually it is concealed by a lining, which may or may not be a "free-hanging" lining.

Using either the basting or the pressing method (see pages 122–123), shape the fold that you want to use. Then, sew this fold in place using a herringbone stitch (page 23).

THE BOUND HEM

This kind of hem is used especially for finishing skirts and pants. It is a sturdy kind of hem. Make sure that you make small stitches so that they remain invisible on the right side of the item.

STEP 1

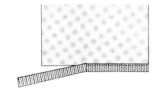

Begin by preshrinking the binding tape to avoid the risk of additional shrinkage when you wash the item. For this reason, you should also make a slight allowance on all your measurements before you cut the length of binding that you want.

STEP 2

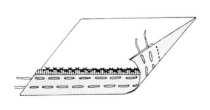

Line up the binding tape edge to edge, with the item on the right side of the fabric. Overlap these edges by ¼ inch, and stitch. Set up the hem with two basted seams. Attach the edge of the binding tape to the fabric with a herringbone stitch (see the top diagram above).

THE CORNERED HEM

This kind of hem is generally found on the bottom of jackets and lined coats. Do not cut the seam allowances; that way, you will be able to make further adjustments in the future.

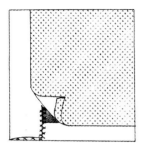

Create the hem on the bottom of the garment by turning the hem fold onto the pieces of facing following the edges of the garment.

Sew the corner or the corners that are created using small herringbone stitches (see the diagram on the left) so that the hem is simultaneously solid and quasi-invisible.

THE CIRCULAR HEM

This kind of hem is found on skirts that are cut on the bias and on tablecloths and other round-shaped items. The hem has either gathers or creases that correspond to the excess fullness. A circular hem consists of one fold, but there are three ways to make it.

1. The Small Hem

Create a simple hem with a reduced height; that way, there will be less excess fabric. Use an iron to create a fold measuring ¼ inch to 1½ inches. Work the tip of the iron from the outer edge toward the interior of the hem to ease in any excess fullness.

2. Using a Gathering Thread

Run a gathering thread by machine or by hand along the edge of the item being hemmed.

Use an iron to create the fold while lightly gathering the edge. Use a pressing cloth to flatten the gathers.

3. The False Hem

Cut a strip along the bias of the fabric that is ⅜ inch in width (see page 222). You can also purchase prefolded bias binding.

Line the edge of the item up with the strip of bias. Stitch within ¼ inch of the edge. Press the seam open with an iron, then turn the false hem under toward the wrong side of the item.

Sew the bias binding ¼ inch in from the edge. Use an iron and a pressing cloth to flatten it. Run a line of basting thread along the top edge of the bias binding and finish it off with a hem stitch.

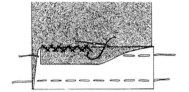

THE DAMASK HEM

This hem allows you to avoid creating a fold that is too thick and gives elasticity to the assembly. It can be used to create elegant articles made with delicate fabrics, like knits.

STEP 1

Create a preliminary fold, then baste by hand using a herringbone stitch or on the sewing machine with a blind hemstitch.

STEP 2

To finish lightweight fabrics, create a simple slipstitch by hand along the edge of the fold. For fabrics that do not fray, use a straight stitch ¼ inch from the edge, then cut along the fold using a pair of pinking shears. On other kinds of fabrics, create a ¼-inch crease along the edge of the fold and stitch 1⁄16 inch from the edge.

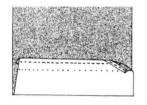

THE FUSIBLE HEM

With the advance of technology, you can now purchase nonwoven strips from the notions shop that can be applied using an iron. The articles that are finished with such strips are machine washable.

STEP 1

The fusible strip should be between 13⁄16 inches and 2 inches in width.

Cut the material to the width you want for the height of the hem. First test to see how the fabric will react.

STEP 2

Make preparations for the first baste. Set the strip between the hem and the wrong side of the article. Keep it in place with a few pins. Set a heated iron over the hem. Do not slide the sole; hold it in place for ten seconds. Then transfer the iron to another section, being sure to slightly overlap with the previous section. Remove the pins as you go along. In case of mistakes, heat up the iron again, remove the hem, and set the strip down again.

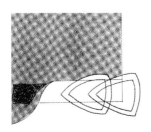

The Kimono

This simple garment can be transformed into a sophisticated piece of indoor attire by the addition of a brocaded silk lining. You can use this trick with other kinds of apparel—for example, a collarless single-breasted jacket, a vest, or even a hooded raincoat.

YOU WILL NEED

Cotton waffle weave, 2⅛ yards by 160 inches wide, in ecru or some other fabric available in wide widths

Silk taffeta, 2⅛ yards by 60 inches wide, in russet; or some other fabric available in wide widths

Sewing thread, in ecru and russet

Basting thread, in a contrasting color

Fine pins

A heavy-duty hanger or a mannequin

Plastic triangle

Yardstick

Tailor's chalk

Dressmaker's scissors

MEASUREMENTS

The kimono is single-breasted and loose-fitting. Take the bust measurement at chest level. Add another 14 inches for fullness, of which 6 inches is for the back width and 4 inches is for each front side.

Then take a measurement for the length of the kimono, which should be the distance between the base of the nape and the crook of the knee.

FABRIC DIMENSIONS

Since the pieces that make up the kimono are rather large, you should make use of fabric in wide widths: 55 inches or 60 inches, according to the material.

The required dimensions are two kimono lengths plus 6 inches for seam and hem allowances.

FABRIC PREPARATION

The waffle weave is an elastic, ribbed fabric. Before you start cutting, make sure you do the following:

–Preshrink the fabric using hot water (it will shrink in length and width by 15% to 20%), and lay it out flat to dry;

–Press both surfaces of the fabric, then leave it on a hanger for 24 hours to stabilize the structure.

To avoid possible discrepancies in how the waffle weave and the lining react to the first washing of the garment, you should also preshrink the fabric that will be used for the lining. This process will allow you to determine how well the colors will "keep" in the long term. If the dyes start to bleed when you rinse the fabric, throw in a handful of coarse salt per liter (or quart) of water used. Lay it out to dry, then press before you begin cutting.

HELPFUL HINTS

The seams of the lining should be lined up exactly over the seams of the body of the kimono. If you do not own a mannequin, you can suspend the work in progress from a hanger. Pin the fabric and its lining together, then baste the two layers of the shoulders and armholes. Attach the edges of the collar to the lining, baste and stitch. Press the seams open with an iron. Turn the garment over onto its right side and press the neckline.

CUTTING THE FABRIC

Each of the pieces in the pattern below includes a ⅝-inch seam allowance and a 1½-inch allowance for the hems at the bottom of the garment.

Fold the waffle weave in half, with the right sides together. Lay the back piece lengthwise along the fabric fold, and position the two front pieces toward the selvages. Next, place the sleeve piece below the two preceding pieces and position the collar center marker over the fabric fold.

Trace along the edges of these pieces with tailor's chalk, the plastic triangle, and the yardstick. Cut along the trace marks. Repeat this process for the taffeta with the same measurements for the pattern pieces.

size 14 kimono

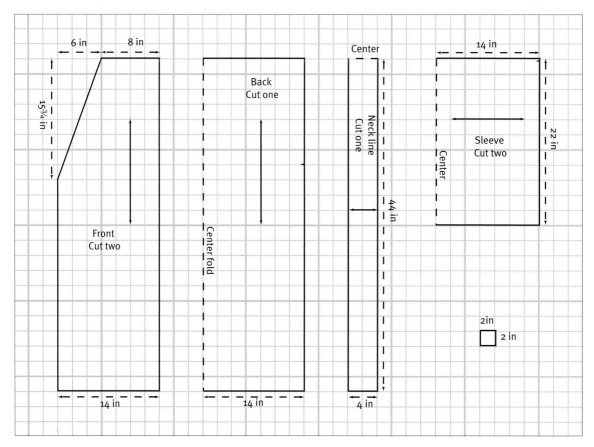

THE KIMONO IN 5 STEPS

Before you begin putting the parts together, carefully overcast all the cut-out pieces of the cotton waffle weave and the silk taffeta that are going to be used in the lining.

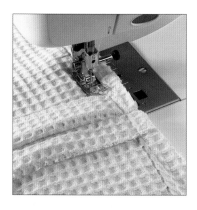

1 JOINING THE SLEEVES

With the right sides of the waffle weave together, lay the two front pieces on top of the back piece. Pin the shoulders together, stitch and press the seams open with an iron.

Unfold your work to lay the sleeves out flat to form one piece extending from the bottom of the back armhole to the bottom of the front armhole.

Place the right sides of the fabrics together, matching the center of the sleeve edge to the shoulder seam. Pin together, then stitch.

2 SETTING THE COLLAR

With the right sides together, pin the side seams to each other and stitch. Still with the right sides together, insert pins into the neckline strip.

Begin attaching the collar by placing the center of the collar piece at the center of the neck edge on the back piece of the kimono.

Stitch the two layers, then press them, turning the seam allowances toward the body of the garment.

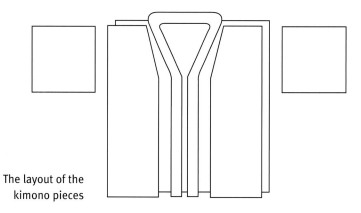

The layout of the kimono pieces

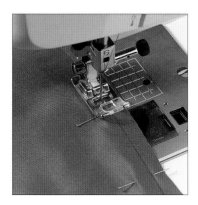

ASSEMBLING THE LINING

Seam shoulders as you did for the kimono; press the seams open. Then join the sleeves as you did for the kimono and press the seams open. Fold the lining at the shoulders with the right sides together. Matching edges, pin and stitch the side seams (including the sleeve edge).

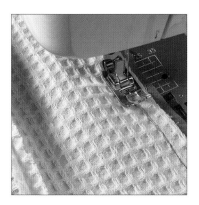

ATTACHING THE LINING TO THE KIMONO

With right sides together, place the lining unit, now assembled, over the kimono unit. Make sure that the corresponding seams of the kimono and the lining are aligned (see the box on page 128).

Stitch the units together along the outer edges of the neck and front opening to hem allowances. Turn the piece right side out, and place the lining sleeves inside the kimono sleeves.

HEMMING

Pressing as necessary, turn the bottom of each sleeve ¾ inch inward so that the raw edges are sandwiched between the waffle weave and the taffeta. Carefully baste this fold, then use the russet-colored thread to stitch it on the right side.

Press the bottom of the kimono and the lining to create 1½ inches inward fold for hems. Pin each fold in place, then stitch. The bottom portions of these two pieces are kept separate to avoid the pulling of the fabric.

FINISHING

You can make a sash from the waffle weave with taffeta lining. To create this addition, cut a long, narrow strip measuring 60 inches by 4 inches from each of the two fabrics.

Place the right sides of the strips together and pin them in place, matching the edges. Stitch, leaving one narrow end of the sash open. Press the seams open with an iron; turn the sash inside out. Close the piece by hand with a running stitch.

Fleece Interlining

PRELIMINARIES

In the example below, the lining is stitched to the top of the main piece. This technique produces a fabric with loft and solidity.

A layer of padding can also be added between the main fabric and the lining. This provides heat-retentive qualities, which is especially desirable in quilts or blankets.

MORE ABOUT THE TECHNIQUE

This technique is also used to add fleece interlinings to apparel like jackets and coats, where heat retention is always a welcome feature, even if nonessential.

Nevertheless, hardiness in the face of inclement weather ultimately depends upon the nature of the garment's main fabric.

STEP 1

Trace a rectangle that circumscribes the completed piece on the wrong side of both the main fabric and the lining. Cut ¾ inch from the trace marks.

Next, trace a rectangle on the sheet of padding or quilt batting. Cut along the trace marks.

STEP 2

Trace along the topstitching lines onto the top layer of fabric with a piece of tailor's chalk or a pencil for light-colored fabric. Or baste. If the motif consists of straight lines, use a yardstick and a plastic triangle. If you would like a more fanciful motif, look for stencils in specialty shops. All you have to do is follow the cutting line with the point of a soft pencil through the grooves of the stencil.

STEP 3

Lay the lining out on a flat surface with the wrong side facing up. Place the sheet of padding centered on top of the lining.

Center it to allow the ¾-inch excess of the lining to extend beyond the sheet on all sides.

While you are working with the batting, especially in Steps 5 and 6 adjacent, support the weight of the piece with your right hand while you guide the fabric with your left. To make the task easier, roll up the unworked part of the piece to reduce the amount of bulk in the way. You can use long headed pins to keep the piece rolled up, but first verify that the pins do not leave marks on the fabric.

A DRESSMAKER'S TRICK

To shorten the process, you can actually skip the basting step in Step 4. You can buy some spray-on adhesive from a notions shop. Lay the sheet of padding out on a large plastic mat; spray the whole surface. Attach the lining to the fleece while smoothing it with the flat of your hand. Turn the piece over and with the padding facing you, coat the surface with glue once again. Lay the main fabric out over the padding. Run a zigzag stitch along the perimeter of the entire piece to fix the three layers in place. Even out the edges.

STEP 4

Lay the main fabric, for the top layer, centered over the sheet of padding with the marker design facing up. Pin the layers together and baste along the edges, stitching through all three layers.

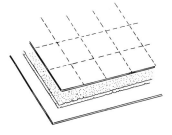

STEP 5

Finish by basting from the center straight out to the edges, then out to the corners. To fit the piece under the arm of the sewing machine more easily, roll up the unworked part of it and secure it with long pins. Stitch the layers together, following the marked design.

STEP 6

Even out the edges. Lay half of a wide piece of bias binding (2 inches in width at a minimum) onto the wrong side of your work. Round out the corners, then turn the second half of the bias binding over onto the right side. Stitch ¼ inch from the edge (see "Attaching Bias Binding" on page 222).

ON THE SEWING MACHINE

For a nice finish to the project, use a thick drapery-type machine thread. Choose a thread in a contrasting color and a size 10 or 11 needle.

Select a thread that matches the lining and load it onto the spool. Attach a quilting foot to the machine. If you do not own such a foot, use a roller foot which can drag the main fabric and lining along simultaneously. Choose the simple straight stitch.

Set the stitch length to about 10 stitches per inch and the machine to average speed.

The Cradle Quilt

The cradle quilt described in this section is made of fabrics that are 100% cotton. It has many features; it is light and warm, washes easily, and dries quickly. It can be used with a wool blanket in the winter. The techniques below can also be used on quilts, bedspreads, and sofa throws. Or you can even use them to create stunning round and square quilted table toppers.

YOU WILL NEED

Cotton fabric, 1⅛ yards by 54 inches wide (for the top of the blanket)

Cotton fabric, 1⅛ yards by 54 inches wide, in the same or in a color that matches the fabric for the topmost layer (for the lining)

Sheet of quilt batting, 60 inches by 40 inches, with ⅜ inch in thickness or loft

Prefolded cotton bias binding, 4½ yards by 2 inches wide (it will be ⅞ inch once folded), in a color that matches the fabric for the topmost layer

Basting thread, in a contrasting color

Sewing thread, in a color that matches the top

Drapery thread, 100% cotton, in a contrasting color

Long, fine pins

Adhesive strip

Plastic triangle

Yardstick

MEASUREMENTS

A blanket for a standard-sized crib measures about 50 inches by 32 inches. However, it is easy to scale these measurements up for a twin bed, or down for a cradle, or to any other bed of your choice.

FABRIC DIMENSIONS

Mark a rectangle measuring 51½ inches by 33½ inches on the main fabric. This is to be used for the topmost layer of the blanket.

Mark a rectangle of the same size from the fabric that you have chosen for the lining.

Also, mark out a rectangle measuring 50 inches by 32 inches on the sheet of quilt batting.

CUTTING THE FABRIC

Cut the pieces out, following the marked edges of the rectangles (which include the seam allowances), from the fabric. Cut out the marked rectangle of batting (which does not include or need a seam allowance).

THE CRADLE QUILT IN 6 STEPS

Once you have cut out the three pieces that will make up the quilt – the top, the lining and the padding (batting) – and before you start putting the parts together, baste to mark where on the top layer the topstitching will go.

1 BASTING THE QUILT DESIGN

Use a basting thread in a contrasting color to establish the three frames whose lines will be used for topstitching the fleece interlining.

The design for this blanket is simple, but delightful and appropriate: It consists of three concentric rectangles.

2 FABRIC AND PADDING PREPARATION

Lay the lining out on a flat surface with the wrong side facing up. Secure the edges of the fabric with the adhesive strip.

Center the sheet of padding over the lining.

Center the top layer over the padding and lining.

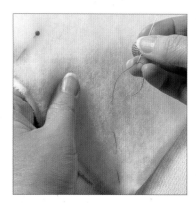

3 BASTING THE LAYERS TOGETHER

By hand and using a different colored basting thread from the design basting, baste the layers together, from the center straight out to the edges, then from the center to each corner.

Pin the edges together and stitch a large zigzag stitch along the perimeter of the piece.

QUILTING

Set the stitch length to ⅛ inch, and use drapery thread for stitching. Work on the center rectangle first, stitching 1/16 inch out from the design basting line. Pivoting at corners, stitch straight lines continuously. If you do stop, knot the thread ends together and work them under the preceding threads.

Working outward, stitch the remaining rectangles.

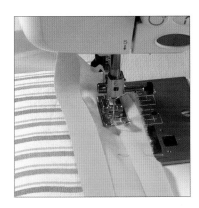

ATTACHING THE BIAS BINDING

Even the edges and round off the corners. Open one edge of the bias binding and align it with the quilt edge on the lining side of the quilt. Carefully stitch the binding around the entire edge, casing around corners.

When you return to the starting point, place the free end over the starting end (already stitched). Allow for an extension of 1 inch to fasten the free end securely.

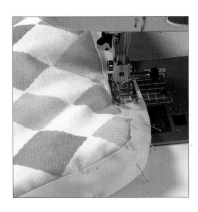

FINISHING THE BIAS BINDING

Fold the remaining half of the bias binding onto the right side of the blanket, stitching around the entire quilt.

Sew ¼ inch from the edge of the bias binding; then remove the basting stitches.

FINISHING

A quilted blanket with padding cannot stand heavy ironing because it would flatten the fleece interlining.

Suspend your blanket from a hanger with clothespins. Place the sole of the iron against the surface and release a few spurts of steam.

Lay the piece flat, and let it cool. This will give the blanket a perfect finish.

Attaching Facings

PRELIMINARIES

Facings, often considered partial linings, are used to finish necklines, the front edges of open garments, and the armhole edges of sleeveless garments.

Facings are generally similar in shape and size to the parts they underline and are cut from the same fabric. The fabric is usually oriented in the same direction as the piece the facing is intended to line.

MORE ABOUT THE TECHNIQUE

A piece of facing is often interfaced; the interfacing may be sew-in or iron-on. Adding the facing requires not only skill but also a great deal of accuracy since its shape must follow the lines of the garment perfectly; it shouldn't be the source of inelegant gathers or seams.

STEP 1

If you are not using iron-on interfacing, presew the interfacing using a long, straight stitch ⅛ inch in from the edge of the facing. A piece of sew-in interfacing subsequently will be joined to the garment when all the pieces are stitched together.

STEP 2

Using a long, straight stitch, sew along the armholes or the neckline of the garment within ¼ inch of the edge to add support to these areas. Try not to pause while stitching.

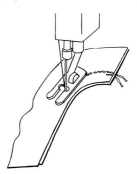

STEP 3

Lay out the facing along the edge of the garment with the right sides together and the assembly markings aligned. Seam the edges.

STEP 4

Turn the facing over and flatten the seam with an iron while directing it toward the inside of the garment. If necessary, trim the seam ¼ inch from the edge. Clip the rounded edges.

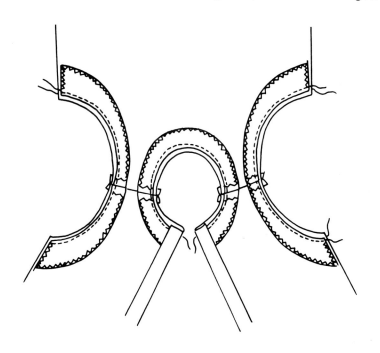

ON THE SEWING MACHINE

For a closed facing, as would be found on a neckline or certain armholes, sew the edges of the facing to the garment. Then flatten with an iron while turning the hem allowances toward the garment.

Stitch as closely as you can to the existing seam, making sure to stitch through all the layers of turned-under edges (the seam allowances and facing, but not the outer garment). This will help hide the facing from the right side of the finished work.

The Single-Breasted Jacket

The pattern for this jacket is unique in that you can use it with any kind of fabric. Because it is single-breasted and somewhat loose-fitting, the jacket goes well with many types of pants and skirts. While it is not lined, this garment is nevertheless durable because the collar and the two front sides are faced.

YOU WILL NEED

Cotton chambray, 1½ yards by 54 inches in width

Sewing thread, in blue

Basting thread, in a contrasting color

Fine pins

Plastic triangle

Yardstick

Dressmaker's chalk

Dressmaker's scissors

HELPFUL HINTS

Prior to adding facing to the jacket, you have to prepare each piece of the garment according to its individual demands and depending upon where and how it fits into the whole. Be sure to complete these preparations if you want a top-quality finished piece.

MEASUREMENTS

Take the bust and hip measurements of the person for whom the garment is being made. Then take the length from the shoulder to the hips and the length from the back of the neck to the hips (see page 247).

Make sure that these measurements match up to those shown on the pattern. If you find any discrepancies, readjust the pattern.

FABRIC DIMENSIONS

For this pattern, the required dimensions for a unidirectional weave is 1¾ yards by 44–45 inches in width or 1½ yards by 54 inches in width.

CUTTING THE FABRIC

The pattern (page 142) includes hem and seam allowances, specifically 1⅜ inches for the hems and ⅝ inch for the seams. Fold the fabric in half so that the selvages line up with one another, and pin the layers together.

Place the pattern pieces for the vest on the wrong side of the fabric. Be sure to pay attention to the straight grain markings. Pin the hem together.

Position the center of the back piece over the fabric fold line. Trace the outline of the pieces as well as the assembly marks. Cut along the trace marks.

Jacket, size 14

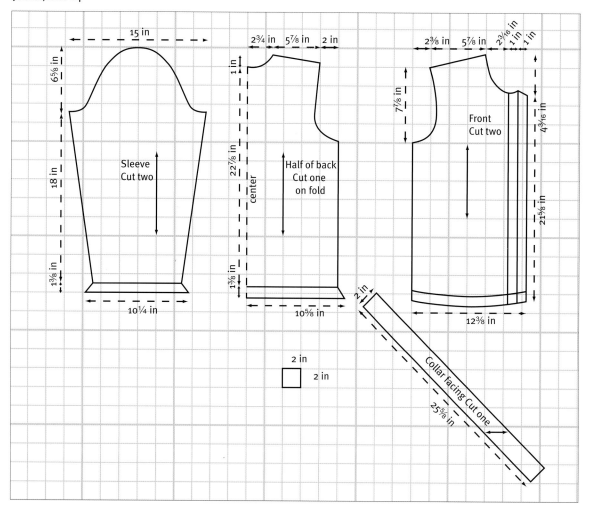

THE JACKET IN 6 STEPS

Carefully overcast all the individual pieces before you start preparing the front and collar facings and before putting everything together.

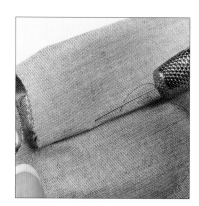

1 PREPARING THE FRONT FACINGS

Following the pattern and, using a light touch of the iron, press the indicated fold line on each of the front facings. Carefully baste along these fold lines.

PREPARING THE COLLAR FACING

With the right sides together, place the two front pieces on the back piece. Pin the shoulders together and stitch ⅝ inch from the edges.

Fold the collar facing in half lengthwise; press the fold with an iron. Position the facing along the neckline, matching the center of the facing to the center back neckline. Pin together, and baste the facing in place.

ATTACHING THE COLLAR FACING

You can sew the collar facing in two stages. Begin at the center back and work forward toward the front edge. Stitch to within ⅜ inch of the edge. Start again at the center back and work the other side to correspond.

Clip the seam allowances. Fold back the front facings, slipping the ends of the collar beneath the front facing on each side of the piece. Press. Topstitch a scant ¼ inch from the neck edge, making sure that you stitch through all layers.

PREPARING THE TWO ARMHOLES

Add support to the sleeve caps by sewing two lines of long, straight stitches ¼ inch in from the edge, beginning and ending the seams as indicated in the diagram below.

Omit backstitches to avoid adding to the thickness of the seam, and let thread ends hang free for the setting of the sleeves.

Maintain the shape of the sleeve head using two rows of stitches.

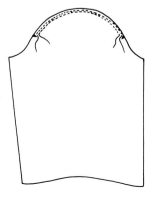

143

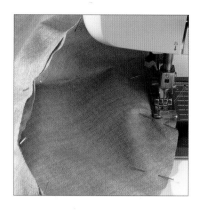

5 SETTING IN THE SLEEVES

Fold the sleeves in half, with right sides together. Pin and stitch the underarm sleeve seams. Press the seams open with an iron.

Set the sleeves into the armholes, right sides together. Spread the gathers out over the opening. Pin together, then stitch. Stitch ⅜ inch from the edge. Notch the seam allowances. Press the excess with an iron so that it runs in the same direction as the sleeves.

6 COMPLETING THE HEMS

Using an iron, turn up a ⅜-inch fold on the bottom of the jacket and also on the ends of the sleeves. Turn up an additional 1-inch fold over the first. Pin and stitch.

Lift the facing up to the same level as the bottom of the jacket so that it covers the hem of the garment. The piece should be as neat as possible, both on the right side as well as the wrong side.

FINISHING

Stitch the jacket a scant ¼ inch in from the edges of the front sides and the sleeve ends using blue thread.

This finishing touch will add an air of discreet elegance to the finished work. There are infinite possibilities here; feel free to replace the blue with any other color of your choice. However, make sure that you use only a dark-colored thread.

5

BUTTON LOOPS, STRAPS, AND ZIPPERS

Rounded Button Loops

PRELIMINARIES

The rounded button loop is a tubular tie sometimes found on the edge of a dress or on a pants waistband as a set of loops to hold a belt in place. Rounded button loops are made from the same fabric used for the garment.

MORE ABOUT THE TECHNIQUE

Oftentimes, clothing and home decor items require the use of small straps so that two separate pieces may be kept in place. These straps do not necessarily serve just a utilitarian purpose; they may also contribute to the finished appearance of a piece. Therefore, think carefully when choosing the most appropriate technique to use. If rounded button loops appeal to you, note that three kinds exist: tubular, embroidered, and bullion stitch embroidered.

THE TUBULAR BUTTON LOOP

STEP 1

On the bias of the fabric, cut out rectangles for as many loops as you intend to make. Each rectangle should measure ¾ inch wide. Its length should be equal to twice the diameter of the button plus an additional ¾ inch.

STEP 2

Fold the piece of bias in half lengthwise, with the right sides together. Gently press the fold without stretching it. Stitch the long edges together within ¼ inch of the edge.

STEP 3

Turn the piece inside out by fastening the knot of a length of thread to one of the seams of the bias and pulling it out through the tube that is formed. Hold the needle by the eye, and push it through using a thimble. Press the piece with an iron to shape a rounded button loop.

STEP 4

Place the button loop on the right side of the fabric, with its end facing out. With the loop tucked between the fabric and its facing, stitch the seam, catching ends in the seam. Turn the facing to the wrong side, with the loop extended at the edge.

THE EMBROIDERED BUTTON LOOP

Embroidered button loops are often used on delicate articles like lingerie. Choose a thread that is appropriate for the fabric.

STEP 1

Secure the end of the thread between the two layers of the button flap with a stitch.

STEP 2

Line up a button with your first stitch, and complete the next stitch on the opposite side of the button. These two stitches mark the points of attachment for the button loop. The distance between these two points should be approximately equal to the diameter of the button, with an additional 1/16 inch for ease.

STEP 3

Complete three or four more passes of the thread adjacent to the first. Using a buttonhole stitch or a blanket stitch, embroider the group of threads that you made.

The knots for these stitches must be located on the outer side of the button loop.

STEP 4

Fasten off the thread at the bottom of the button loop by running two backstitches through the button flap.

THE BULLION STITCH EMBROIDERED BUTTON LOOP

This type of button loop is meant to complement the small mother-of-pearl buttons traditionally used on fine lingerie and clothes for new-born infants.

STEP 1

Thread a needle. Secure the end of the thread between the two layers of the button flap.

STEP 2

Take the needle up through the edge of the button flap to create a short backstitch. Leave the needle in the fabric with its point directed upward.

Wind the thread counterclockwise around the needle (see the adjacent illustration).

Continue winding the thread until you obtain a length of winding that is equal to the diameter of the button plus $1/16$ inch.

STEP 3

Hold the wound-up part of the thread between your thumb and index finger, and pull the rest of the thread through it.

STEP 4

Finish by attaching the button loop with backstitches, each of which should be set at an equal distance from the edge of the button.

ON THE SEWING MACHINE

Secure one of the ends of the tubular button loop by lightly flaring the stitch outward. This simple step will make it easier to turn the button loop inside out, and it will also give you a loop that is clean, symmetrical, and less likely to crease.

You should take this precautionary measure even with fine, light-weight fabrics – especially if the tube shaped for the button loop is narrow. Remember that fine fabric is also delicate fabric.

Holed button

BUTTONS

The button is both a decorative and a functional accessory. Choose your buttons according to the type of fabric you are using and the effect you desire. Thick fabrics support larger buttons.

The quality and thickness of the thread that you use to attach the button depends upon the size of the button, its shape, and the composition of the fabric that backs it.

Novelty buttons

Varieties of Buttons

Two- and four-holed buttons are used with fabrics of thin or average thickness.

Shank buttons, many of which are made from metal, are usually used with thicker fabrics.

Buttons that require a fabric covering usually consist of two parts that are snapped together after the top piece (the cap or shell) has been covered with the fabric of your choice. The edges of the fabric covering are held inside the button after the two parts are snapped together.

Shank button

Button Sizes

In the notions shop you can find buttons of all sorts of colors, shapes, and sizes, though most buttons are usually between ¼ inch and 2½ inches in diameter.

Here are a few guidelines to help you choose the appropriate button, depending upon the style and the size of your article:
— Men's shirts = ½-inch buttons
— Women's blouses = 9/16-inch buttons
— Dresses or dress coats = 5⁄8-inch or ¾-inch buttons
— Women's and men's blazers = ¾-inch to ⅞-inch buttons
— Coats = buttons wider than 1 inch

Button Choice

Large buttons are frequently used as sewing decoration, though not on pillowcases or covers. For them, choose more comfortable small four-holed buttons if the pillows are to be used for back or head rests.

Find out all you can about the composition of buttons when you make your purchase. Some cannot be washed or dry-cleaned.

This is usually the case for buttons that are used in braids and trimmings, buttons that are covered in fur, buttons made of some metals, and buttons made of nonvarnished wood. You will have to remove these buttons before you wash or clean the item they adorn and reattach them afterward. Limit your use of these buttons to items that do not require regular maintenance.

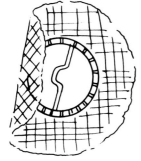

Covered button

The Lingerie Bag

Made from an elegant, silky fabric, this bag is as stylish as it is easy to put together. Using the pattern below as a point of departure, you can create all sorts of bags or cases for storing handkerchiefs, slippers, underwear, table napkins, and more. These bags are painless to wash and should fit easily into a suitcase. Their lightweight and practical nature should come in handy for those who are always on the run.

YOU WILL NEED

Striped silk taffeta, a 27½-inch by 15¾-inch rectangle
Cotton bias binding, 12½ inches by 1 inch wide, in a color that matches the main fabric
Sewing thread, in a color that matches the main fabric
Basting thread, in a contrasting color
Thick cotton thread, for making button loops
Five buttons for covering, ⅜ inch in diameter each
Pliers, for closing the buttons
Fine pins
Regular pencil
Yardstick
Plastic triangle

MEASUREMENTS
Take your measurements for the bag (height, width, breadth) taking into consideration the size, shape, and weight of the accessories that it will hold.

The dimensions of the finished bag will depend on these measurements.

FABRIC DIMENSIONS
For the lingerie bag shown in the photograph on the opposite page, you will need a fabric rectangle measuring 27½ inches by 15¾ inches, enough for the large rectangle that forms the bag itself with leftover scraps to make the button loops and button coverings (see the pattern on page 152).

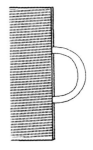

HELPFUL HINTS

Choose a fabric that has a texture and color that are well-suited for the items your bag will hold. If the bag will hold fragile or delicate items and will be used out in the open, select a fine piece of fabric. On the other hand, if the bag will stay in your closet or be put in a suitcase, you can use a fabric that comes in neutral colors and still obtain tasteful results.

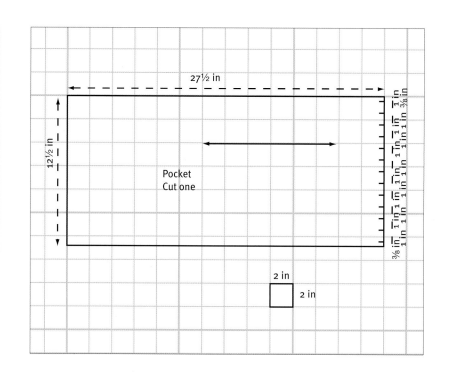

27½ in

12½ in

Pocket
Cut one

⅜ in 1 in 1 in 1 in 1 in 1 in 1 in ⅜ in

2 in

2 in

THE LINGERIE BAG
IN 4 STEPS

This project offers the elegance of silk, the festiveness of color, the delicacy of fine fabric, and the simplicity of form. The added extra of button loops makes this bag irresistible.

PREPARING THE BUTTON LOOPS

On the straight grain of the wrong side of the fabric, use the plastic triangle and the yardstick to trace out a rectangle measuring 27½ inches by 12½ inches.

On the bias of the fabric scraps, trace out five rectangles measuring 3 inches by 1⅜ inches for the button loops. On the straight grain, trace five 2-inch-sided squares for the button fabric coverings.

Overcast the outline of the rectangle that forms the main piece of the bag. Make a ⅜-inch-wide double-folded hem around the perimeter of the piece.

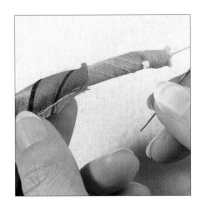

MAKING THE BUTTON LOOPS

With the right sides together, fold the rectangles in half lengthwise for the button loops. Pin the folds and stitch ¼ inch in from the long edges. Trim the seam allowances to ⅛ inch from the seam.

Draw a needle threaded with thick cotton thread through the button loop fabric at an angle. Pull the needle, eye first, through the tube that is created. Turn the right side of the button loop piece out, then stretch it and use an iron to give it a more rounded shape. Repeat this procedure for each button loop.

ATTACHING THE BUTTON LOOPS

Fold the big fabric rectangle, wrong sides in and ends overlapping, into three unequal parts to create an envelope measuring 13¾ inches by 11¾ inches. Stitch ¼ inch from the edges.

Lay the button loops out along the edge that will serve as the flap for the bag, spacing them evenly along this edge.

Place the ends of the button loops extending outward toward the outer edge. Pin them in place, then baste. (The photograph shows the position of the loop when it is finished.)

JOINING THE FACING

With the right sides of the fabrics together, place the bias over the end of the loop, sandwiching them. Turning under the short ends of the binding to conceal raw edges, pin the long edge of the binding to the bag. Topstitch ¹⁄₁₆ inch in from the bias edge, sewing through all layers and catching loop ends in the seam. Turn the bias to inside and press. The button loops now extend outward. Topstitch ¹⁄₁₆ inch from the seam to keep the bias in place.

FINISHING

With a pencil, trace the outlines of the button caps onto the wrong sides of the remaining squares of fabric. Fasten a gathering thread a ¼ inch from the edge of the outline. Position the button cap in the interior so that the rounded face is against the fabric.

Tighten the thread and knot it. Cut the fabric ¹⁄₁₆ inch from the gathering seam. Snap the base of the button onto the cap so that the edges of the fabric covering are caught in between. Push the two pieces together as hard as you can, using a pair of pliers if needed.

Mitered Button Loops

PRELIMINARIES

A mitered button loop is made from a strip of fabric or a piece of flat binding in a color that matches the main fabric.

It consists of a solid strap and is often found in decorative items, though it may also be used to complement a garment. It is called a mitered button loop because it resembles the miter that you might find on a bishop's headdress.

MORE ABOUT THE TECHNIQUE

In appearance, the mitered button loop is much flatter than the rounded button loop, but it is also more prominent. It is suitable for modern apparel and home decor items as well as accessories intended for daily use. Its appeal lies in the practical applications it has to offer; this loop can be used to close, clasp, or hold together decorative items.

STEP 1

Prepare a strip of straight grain fabric. Fold it once to create a 90-degree angle, then again to form the other side of the button loop.

The center of the button loop should be opposite the pointed corner that is created.

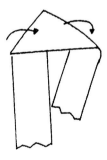

STEP 2

On the wrong side of the fabric and below the bottom of the mitered loop, close off the loop opening using three backstitches.

These stops, which will be concealed beneath the flap, help prevent the point of the button loop from becoming misshapen after a button is secured to it.

STEP 3

The length of the loop should equal the diameter of the button plus an additional ⅛ inch so that the button can pass through, and an additional 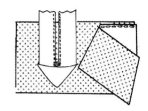 ¼ inch so that it can be attached. Position the mitered button loop toward the edge of the flap with the corner pointing in.

STEP 4

Lay out the piece of lining that is to be used for the button flap (see "Linings," Chapter 4).

Stitch along the edge of the flap while holding the fabric, the lining, and the edges of the mitered loop together.

STEP 5

Turn the button flap inside over onto its right side and topstitch the interior edges of the loop (or loops, if there are several) at a distance of 1/16 inch from the opening. The point of this is to strengthen the strip that is formed.

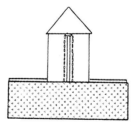

ON THE SEWING MACHINE

The thread stop on the tip of the mitered button loop should be especially clean and secure. To make sure that this is the case, set the sewing machine on "slow" and complete a straight stitch with a length of 1/16 inch.

When you come to the corner at the tip of the miter, let the needle remain fixed in the fabric. Lift the presser foot, pivot the button loop around the needle, and then lower the presser foot once again. Carefully continue stitching the seam.

ATTACHING BUTTONS

Attaching Two- or Four-Holed Buttons

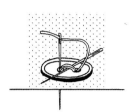

The properly attached button should not make contact with the surface of the fabric. Allow for a gap of at last 1/16 inch to anticipate the thickness of the fabric around the buttonhole opening(s).

Thread a needle and knot it at the end. Lay a matchstick or a tapestry needle across the button. Take the needle up through the wrong side of the fabric. Then guide the needle through one of the holes of the button. Take the needle back down through another hole while crossing over the matchstick (or the thick needle). Repeat this process three or four times to sew the button securely in place. The thread must traverse four-holed buttons in a parallel manner.

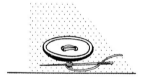

Remove the matchstick or the thick needle and pull the button upward to disengage the shank created by the stitchwork. Take the thread down through the button and wind the thread around the shank several times. Complete two or three backstitches on the wrong side to finish off the thread.

Another technique consists of setting the length of the shank by folding the fabric and positioning the button on the bias, right next to its point of attachment. Stitch or sew as you did before, taking the thread through the holes of the button. Secure the thread using two or three backstitches on the wrong side of the fabric.

Attaching Button Reinforcements

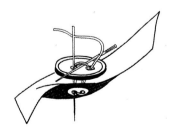

A few of the more delicate varieties of fabric require a reinforcing button. Reinforcing buttons is also useful with buttons that undergo great strain. The point of attachment for the button can be reinforced by a little square (or rectangle) cut from the fabric of your item or by another button that is somewhat less in diameter than the main button.

Thread a needle, then sew the button on as described above, but bind it to the reinforcing fabric square or button on the wrong side of the fabric.

Another possible technique involves applying a piece of iron-on material onto the wrong side of the button's point of attachment. If you decide to use this method, make sure that the iron-on reinforcement is not visible from the right side of the article.

Attaching Buttons by Machine

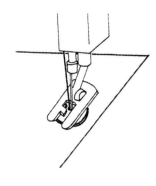

A few sewing machines offer a button attachment feature. This can only be used to attach buttons with holes.

Install the special button presser foot to the machine. Position the needle slightly to the left and off-center. Pull back the feed dogs of the machine or set the stitch length to zero; set the zigzag stitch length to between ⅛ inch to ¼ inch, depending upon the distance between the holes of the button.

Make four or five stitches through each hole and finish off by knotting the two threads together on the wrong side of the fabric.

Attaching Shank Buttons

Thread a needle with button thread and knot it at the end. Take the needle up through the wrong side of the fabric and pull it through the shank of the button. Lay the shank of the button onto the right side of the flap; restitch along the side.

Repeat three or four times before fastening the thread with several backstitches on the wrong side of the button flap.

Positioning Buttons

You sew on a button only after the buttonhole has been completed. Line up the two parts of the closure edges as accurately as you can. Hold the structure in place with a few pins.

Thrust the tip of a piece of tailor's chalk or a pencil through the buttonhole and mark out the precise location of the button. Attach the button using these marks.

The Work Bag

Hang it on the walls of children's rooms as a receptacle for crayons and other accessories, in the bathroom for your hygiene and personal care products, or by the doorway for your keys and unread mail; this work bag is bound to find a good place in your home. It is suitable for many purposes, some of which are more useful than others; but despite its functional design, this work bag is not the least bit lacking in elegance.

YOU WILL NEED

Cotton pique for the backing, 19¾ inches by 15¾ inches, in violet
Cotton pique for the four pockets, 15¾ inches by 19¾ inches, in anise
Prefolded cotton bias binding, 3¼ yards by ⅞ inch wide, in violet
Sewing thread, in two colors – violet and anise
Fine pins
Four buttons of an appropriate diameter
Plastic triangle
Yardstick
Tailor's chalk
Dressmaker's scissors

MEASUREMENTS

Whether you follow the pattern on page 160 exactly or decide to construct the work bag according to your own measurements, be sure to respect the following principles: Use a sturdy fabric for the backing, and allow for a layer of lining if any side of the bag measures more than 19¾ inches in length.

The number of pockets can vary, depending upon their intended use and the size of the bag.

FABRIC DIMENSIONS

The bag that appears in the photograph on the opposite page features a rectangular backing that measures 19¾ inches by 15¾ inches and pockets that each measure 7½ inches long by 6¼ inches wide.

CUTTING THE FABRIC

Fold but do not cut the piece of violet cotton pique into four. Line up the corners of the fabric, then cut to create equally rounded corners.

On the wrong side of the anise cotton pique, use the yardstick and the set square to trace out four rectangles for the pockets that measure 9 inches by 7 inches each. These pieces should be on the straight grain. Cut them out by following the trace marks.

Finally, cut nine strips for the button loops from the prefolded bias, making each strip 3⅛ inches in length.

HELPFUL HINTS

The pattern for the work bag included here is a standard design. However, you can easily use your own measurements. Select sizes for the pockets depending upon what accessories you want to put in them. For the dimensions of the backing, give some thought to the place or the board where the work bag will hang – take this into consideration only if the measurements provided here are not to your liking.

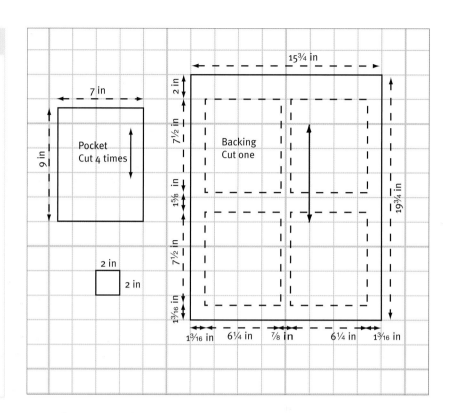

Pocket
Cut 4 times

7 in
9 in

2 in
2 in

15¾ in
2 in
7½ in
1⅝ in
7½ in
1³⁄₁₆ in
19¾ in

Backing
Cut one

1³⁄₁₆ in   6¼ in   ⅞ in   6¼ in   1³⁄₁₆ in

THE WORK BAG
IN 4 STEPS

Before you move onto the steps below, carefully overcast all the pieces that you have cut out to protect the edges from possible unraveling.

1
PREPARING THE MITERED BUTTON LOOPS

Fold the nine pieces of bias binding to shape the miters of the button loops. Four of them will be attached to the pockets and five will be sewn to the top of the backing so that the bag can be hung from the wall.

Insert a pin into the miter of each button loop to keep the fold in place. Use the tip of an iron to reinforce the folds.

2 SEWING THE MITER OF THE BUTTON LOOP

Set your sewing machine on "slow" and prepare to complete a straight stitch with a length of $\frac{1}{16}$ inch. Stitch across the center $\frac{1}{4}$ inch of the miter to hold the folds in place.

If desired, carefully stitch along the miter of each button loop (see page 155 for how to pivot around the corner).

Lay out the violet bias binding around the perimeter of the backing.

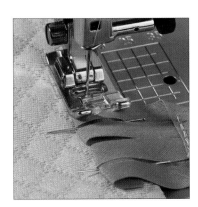

3 ATTACHING THE BUTTON LOOPS

Use the iron to create a $1\frac{1}{8}$-inch hem fold along the top of each of the pockets and a $\frac{3}{8}$-inch fold on each of the three other sides.

Baste the folds, then pin a button loop onto the edge of each pocket. Set the ends of each button loop into the pocket about 1 inch from the opening edge.

Attach five button loops to the top of the backing: one in the center, one at each end and two others evenly spaced between the first three.

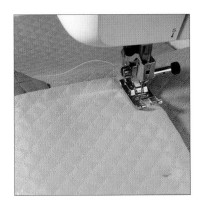

4 ATTACHING BUTTON LOOPS AND THE POCKETS TO THE BACKING

Stitch the button loops 0.20 inch from the edge of the pockets and the backing. Use a double stitch to strengthen the seams. Next pin the pockets onto the violet backing following the pattern measurements or your own plan.

Sew sides and bottom edges, using straight stitch with the stitch length set to a scant $\frac{1}{8}$ inch.

FINISHING

Sew in a button to the backing at each pocket button loop so that the pockets can be closed, but do so only if you want this feature. You do not have to do this for the loops on top of the backing; these will only be used to hang the work bag.

Tack hooks on the wall where you want to hang your piece, then ease the hooks through the openings of the loops on the top of the bag.

The Zipper

PRELIMINARIES

The zipper is a mechanism that consists of two strips of fabric each bordered by a row of interlocking metal or plastic teeth. It has a slider that allows for the two strips to close or open. The teeth are interlocking.

While a zipper can be useful on an article of clothing, it may go well with a decorative piece too.

MORE ABOUT THE TECHNIQUE

How you apply a zipper has a lot to do with what kind of finishing you desire; it might be exposed or it might be concealed by a flap. A third option is also available. A separating zipper makes it possible for the two sides of a garment to be completely separated from each other when opened down to the base; this can turn out to be very practical for a vest, a jacket, or an anorak.

CHOOSING THE ZIPPER

Zippers are available in a variety of lengths and colors. The teeth that run along the two strips of fabric generally come in either plastic or metal. Each of these materials offers its own set of advantages. You should make your choice depending on the nature of the article you are working on.

Here are a few useful notes for your reference when purchasing a zipper:
— for skirts or pants: choose a plastic or a metal zipper that is usually 7 inches long;
— for necklines: choose a plastic or a metal zipper that is 5 inches long;
— for pockets: choose a plastic or a metal zipper that is 5 inches long;
— for the back openings of dresses: choose a plastic or a metal zipper that is 20 to 22 inches long;
— for jackets: choose a plastic or a metal zipper that is 18 inches to 20 inches long;
— for cushion cases: choose a plastic or a metal zipper that is 12 inches long;

Only zippers that are made of plastic can be shortened. If you do have to reduce the length, wrap a piece of adhesive tape around the zipper at the point where you want to cut it. Cut off the piece you do not want with the scissors and then apply the zipper. Stitch along both of the edges, but make sure that you also stitch along the cut end in order to assure that the whole zipper is firmly fixed in place.

In the case of a metal zipper on the other hand, make sure that you do not stitch through the teeth regardless of the length of the zipper and the size of the teeth.

When you press the piece do not place the iron directly over the zipper regardless of whether it is made of metal or plastic. Place a pressing cloth between the zipper and the sole of the iron.

If it becomes difficult to slide the zipper open and closed after washing, here's another useful tip to consider: run a dry piece of soap or a stick of paraffin down the underside of the zipper while it is closed. If the teeth have not been damaged, the zipper should be as good as new.

ATTACHING A CENTERED ZIPPER

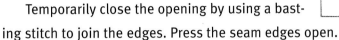

STEP 1

The opening itself must be about ¾ inch longer than the zipper teeth section.

Temporarily close the opening by using a basting stitch to join the edges. Press the seam edges open.

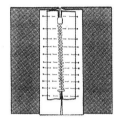

STEP 2

Pin the closed zipper into place on the wrong side of the main article. Baste it in, but make sure to check that the centerline of the zipper lines up precisely with the center of the anticipated opening.

STEP 3

Install the zipper foot on the sewing machine. Stitch along the right side of the article ¼ inch from the basted shut edge of the opening.

STEP 4

Start stitching on one side of the opening; begin at the bottom of the zipper and sew toward the top. Fasten off the thread.

Start again at the bottom of the zipper on the other side of the opening. Set the fabric at a right angle and complete a couple of crosswise stitches to fasten the entire zipper in place. Stitch along the other side of the opening from the bottom to top. This helps avoid the formation of gaps.

ON THE SEWING MACHINE

The metal zipper (cording) foot is narrow and notched on both sides, allowing you to stitch close to the zipper teeth. The needle should pass through the notch on the side of the foot closest to the zipper. The notch assures that the needle will not hit the teeth if you allow the feed dogs to guide the work smoothly.

ATTACHING A LAPPED ZIPPER

STEP 1

Open the zipper and place it face down over the basted seam. Baste, then stitch one side of the zipper tape to the back seam allowance only (not through the outer fabric).

STEP 2

Close the zipper. Turn the zipper face up. Press the attached fabric away from the zipper. Baste the same zipper tape just sewn under the pressed fabric and sew along the edge of the fabric, attaching the zipper tape a second time.

STEP 3

Lay the zipper flat and face down over the basted seam; baste the free zipper tape to the fabric. Sew the second side of the zipper in place. Because the zipper is not centered at the seam, the placket side covers the zipper completely.

STEP 4

End with diagonal stitching at the bottom of the placket to join the two vertical lines of stitching.

ATTACHING A SEPARATING ZIPPER
STEP 1

Open and separate entirely the two parts of the separable zipper.

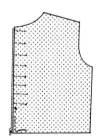

STEP 2

Pin each of these parts to the edge of your item and baste. Reattach the slider for the zipper.
Check that your whole item is lined up perfectly. Then open up the separable zipper once again.

STEP 3

Stitch along the right side of the fabric. On each side, begin on the bottom of the zipper and move toward the top.

The Tote Bag

A zipper can go with all sorts of items. It is a very practical way to allow two pieces of fabric to lock temporarily to form a tight compartment protected from light, dust, and the elements. The tote bag presented in this section is an ideal place for you to store your sewing work, groceries, or baby supplies. It is made from thick cotton and is therefore quite durable and machine washable.

YOU WILL NEED

Cotton canvas, 1⅛ yards by 44–45 inches wide
Thick iron-on or fusible interfacing, 1⅛ yards by 44–45 inches wide, in white
Plastic zipper, in ecru
Sewing thread for strong seams, in ecru
Yardstick
Plastic triangle
Dressmaker's chalk
Fine pins
Dressmaker's scissors

HELPFUL HINTS

If you decide to use your own measurements, make sure that these are on the large side so that you can easily slip documents in and out without needing to fold them.

MEASUREMENTS
The finished bag should measure 15¾ inches in length by 12 inches in height by 4 inches in breadth.
    Each of the straps should measure 40 inches by 2 inches.
    The zipper used is an ordinary, nonseparable zipper measuring 22 inches in length.

FABRIC DIMENSIONS
Feel free to alter the dimensions of the bag so that it will fit the documents and accessories that you want it to hold. To make these allowances, you can simply lengthen or shorten the two front pieces as well as the strips that will be used for the front and back gussets.

CUTTING THE FABRIC
On the wrong side of the printed cotton fabric, trace the outlines of the pattern pieces of the tote bag (see the pattern on page 166). Cut out the fabric pieces ⅜ inch beyond the trace marks.
    Trace the outlines of the same pattern pieces onto the fusible interfacing and then cut out the fabric pieces along the trace marks.
    Symmetrically round off the corners of the two front fabric pieces using a pair of scissors.

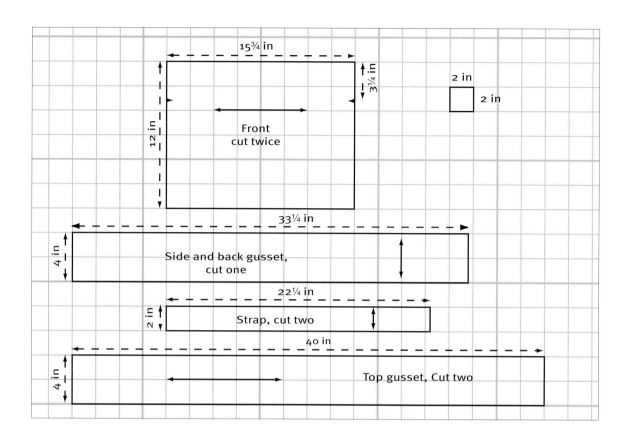

15¾ in

3¼ in

12 in

Front
cut twice

2 in

2 in

33¼ in

4 in

Side and back gusset,
cut one

22¼ in

2 in

Strap, cut two

40 in

4 in

Top gusset, Cut two

THE TOTE BAG
IN 4 STEPS

Apply the fusible interfacing to the back of each piece using an iron. Then overcast the borders of the interfaced pieces before you begin putting the bag together.

ATTACHING THE ZIPPER AND PREPARING THE STRAPS

In anticipation of a layer of lining, use the iron to create a fold along the edges of the top gusset pieces. Baste the zipper from end to end between these two pieces. Set the zipper foot into the sewing machine and start sewing.

Use the iron to press a ⅜-inch hem fold along the edges of the wrong side of each strap. Baste them and then use the tip of the iron to fold each strip in half lengthwise. The folded straps should measure 1¾ inches in width.

ATTACHING THE STRAPS

After folding the straps, stitch them lengthwise ¼ inch from the edges. Fold one strap over to form an inverted U. Pin the ends of the strap to one front fabric piece so the outer edge of the strap is 2⅜ inches in from each side of the back.

With the loose center forming a handle, allow the ends to extend ⅝ inch below the bottom edge; they will be caught later in the gusset seam.

Stitch both sides of the strap, backstitching 2⅜ inches from the top of the bag to strengthen the point of attachment. Attach the second strap to the remaining front piece in the same way.

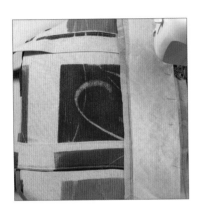

ATTACHING THE BACK GUSSET

With right sides togetherand with the zipper closed, pin one of the top gusset pieces onto one of the front fabric pieces of the bag. Baste, then stitch

Do the same for the remaining top gusset and the other front fabric piece. Reach inside to open the zipper before completing the gusset. Pin the ends of the two gusset pieces in place and adjust their lengths. Stitch, then cut off any excess fabric. Flatten the seams with an iron and turn the bag to the right side.

ATTACHING THE BACK GUSSET

With right sides together, lay the back gusset over the edges of one front piece, matching center bottoms.

Turn your work so the gusset is on top, make it easier to round the corners as you stitch (see page 65 for this technique). Catch the strap ends in the seam.

Join gusset to the other front in the same way. Press the seams open with an iron and carefully notch the seam allowances near the rounded corners.

FINISHING

Open the zipper completely to make sure that the tote bag can easily be turned onto its right side or its wrong side. Do this prior to mending or washing the bag. This simple step also gives your zipper a longer life.

Check one last time that the pieces that make up the bag are symmetrical and balanced, and reshape. Your tote bag is now ready for the road.

Buttonholes

PRELIMINARIES

Buttonholes can be created either by hand or by machine. These finishing touches are not difficult to carry out, but they require a lot of attention to detail and must be completed using high-quality thread.

Buttonholes are the target of much pulling and stretching and thus should be sturdily tailored so that they do not twist out of shape or warp with use.

MORE ABOUT THE TECHNIQUE

To simplify the process of determining how to space out the buttonholes, lay out an odd number of buttons onto your item. Fold the section where the buttons will be attached in half crosswise; then insert a pin into the fold for use as a point of reference.

Continue to fold and mark the section successively in halves, proceeding from both sides of the first pin. Fold the remaining spans in half, inserting marker pins as you go along.

DETERMINING THE LENGTH OF THE BUTTONHOLE

Technique A

To find out what the proper length of a buttonhole should be, measure the diameter of the button it is meant to fit. Add the thickness of the button and $\frac{1}{16}$ inch of ease to this figure.

Technique B

Use a narrow ribbon or a flat strap. Wrap a piece of the ribbon around the button at its widest point. Use the felt-tip pen to mark this exact diameter on the ribbon. The final measurement should be equal to the diameter + the thickness of the button + $\frac{1}{16}$ inch of ease.

Retain the ribbon so that you can measure the other buttonholes. Use basting thread to mark out the vertical center of the button flap.

Determine the lengths of the intervals between buttonholes and trace them out with a piece of tailor's chalk.

THE TWO VARIETIES OF BUTTONHOLES

The Horizontal Buttonhole

Known for its ability to withstand tension, this kind of buttonhole lies perpendicular to the edge of the garment. The button is positioned toward the outer edge of the buttonhole. This kind of buttonhole is usually used on thick, tough, or rough fabrics.

The Vertical Buttonhole

Known for its ability to secure a closure, this buttonhole is usually used with fabrics that are more lightweight. It is parallel to the edge of the garment and is generally set along the center of the button flap. When fastened, the button lodges squarely in the center of the buttonhole.

THE VERTICAL HAND-EMBROIDERED BUTTONHOLE

This buttonhole is made by working through all the layers of the button flap.

Thread a needle with a thread that is appropriate for this kind of work.

STEP 1

Delineate the edges of the buttonhole with a tiny running stitch, then cut the opening for the hole. Make sure that you do not cut through the threads of the outline just sewn.

STEP 2

With the thread, work buttonhole stitches around the opening, covering the running stitches made previously.

STEP 3

At each end, complete three or four stitches that are perpendicular to the buttonhole opening. Rework these threads using a buttonhole stitch, with the knots directed toward the opening, but make sure not to catch the fabric in these end stitches.

POINTS OF DETAIL

While the seam ripper is a very practical tool that can be used in many different situations, you should also consider opening up a button-hole with a craft knife. To do so, lay out your item flat with the buttonhole perpendicular to you. Set the point of the knife blade at the top of the buttonhole and push down. Proceed gently and repeat as many times as necessary. Make sure that you do not damage any of the stitches that border the buttonhole opening.

A DRESSMAKER'S TRICK

On some lightweight or loose fabrics like knits, you have to strengthen the fabric by set-ting a piece of cloth beneath it where you plan to make your buttonhole. Baste a rec-tangular piece of cloth whose sides extend ⅜ inch beyond from the perimeter of the actual buttonhole onto the fabric. This will give it shape when it comes time to do embroidery work. This tech-nique is as useful for hand-tailored buttonholes as it is for those that are machine-tailored. The piece of sup-porting cloth can be con-cealed if you apply a layer of facing to it. However, if you are not going to face, trim the piece down to the edges of the finished buttonhole.

THE HORIZONTAL HAND-EMBROIDERED BUTTONHOLE

You prepare this type of buttonhole the same way you did for the one described in the previous section.

Then continue with the three steps that follow.

STEP 1

Work along the one edge of the buttonhole opening using a button-hole stitch. Embroider the end of the buttonhole that is closer to the outer edge of the flap; fan the stitches out.

STEP 2

Continue embroidering as you did before, but along the other, opposing edge of the buttonhole opening.

STEP 3

Finish up on the other end of the buttonhole by completing three or four stitches that are perpendicular to the buttonhole opening.

Embroider through these threads using a buttonhole stitch, with the knots directed toward the opening, but make sure that they do not catch the fabric.

THE MACHINE-EMBROIDERED BUTTONHOLE

If your sewing machine does not already provide a mechanism for making buttonholes, this is the best way to proceed:

STEP 1

Mark out the length of the buttonhole on your item with a piece of tailor's chalk.

Position the needle on the machine slightly to the left and off-center.

STEP 2

Prepare the sewing machine for a zigzag stitch with a width of 1/16 inch and a length that is between 0.00 inch and 1/32 inch.

Set the satin stitch foot into the machine.

STEP 3

Embroider one side of the buttonhole. When completing the last three or four stitches, set the stitch width to ⅛ inch. Leave the needle in the fabric and pivot your item around it.

STEP 4

When you start embroidering the other side of the buttonhole, set the stitch width back to ¹⁄₁₆ inch. After you finish embroidering this side, lift the needle, set the width to ⅛ inch and once again complete three or four stitches to finish off the other end of the buttonhole.

Carefully run a seam ripper down the intended buttonhole opening to finish.

USING THE MACHINE BUTTONHOLER

If your sewing machine comes with a buttonhole-making feature, it will be able to automatically embroider both sides and the ends of the buttonhole.

Using a piece of tailor's chalk, begin by marking out the exact location of the buttonhole.

Activate the buttonholer for your machine, then set the stitch width and length for a satin stitch.

Press down on the pedal and let the machine automatically complete the embroidery work. Cut open the buttonhole opening with a seam ripper.

ON THE SEWING MACHINE

On an electric sewing machine that offers such a mechanism, you will find a wide array of possible buttonhole designs that range from the classical to the downright fanciful.

Whatever buttonhole design you happen to choose, your sewing machine should be able to give an even and durable embroidered finish. The only requirement that you must follow is to choose a thread and a needle that are appropriate for the type of fabric you are using.

The Child's Jacket

Made from fleece, the child's jacket presented here is not only lightweight, warm, and snug, but also easy to make. Your little ones will be delighted if you choose to add a few novelty buttons to the pattern prescribed. But you should know that this cardigan can be fitted to individuals of any size, including adults. Purchase sufficient fabric and feel free to use buttons and add finishing touches that are age-appropriate.

YOU WILL NEED

Fleece, ⅞ yard by 54 inches wide, in ecru

Loop pile fleece, ⅜ yard by 54 inches wide, in red

Sewing thread, in two colors: ecru and red

Basting thread, in a contrasting color

Six novelty shank buttons for children's clothing

Seam ripper for opening buttonholes

Yardstick

Plastic triangle

Tailor's chalk

Fine pins

Dressmaker's scissors

MEASUREMENTS

Take down the bust and hip measurements. Then take the length from the shoulder to the hips and the length from the back of the neck to the hips.

Make sure that these measurements match up well to those shown on the pattern. If this is not the case, correct the dimensions of pieces that might pose a problem before you start cutting.

FABRIC DIMENSIONS

You will need a piece of fabric that is without nap that measures 1 yard by 44–45 inches in width or ⅞ yard by 54 inches in width.

THE FRONT BAND

The front band or overlap of a garment should be compatible with the size of the buttons. You should widen or reduce it depending upon the diameter of the buttons. The minimum width of the front band should be half the diameter of a button plus ¼ inch. For example, if your button is 1 inch across, you will need to create a front band that is ½ inch + ¼ inch = ¾ inch in width.

In addition, make sure that you do not neglect to follow the conventions concerning button placement: for girls, the button flap goes on the left, and for boys, the right.

HELPFUL HINTS

Shank buttons are easier to attach than other buttons; their buttonholes are also easier to make. Regardless of whether you use classic or novelty shank buttons, both of which go quite well for this sort of jacket, you should know that traditional two- or four-holed buttons are still an option.

CUTTING THE FABRIC

The pattern below includes hem as well as seam allowances: The hem allowances measure 1⅜ inches and the seam allowances measure ⅝ inch, or in some cases ⅜ inch.

Fold each of the fabrics in half with right sides in and line the selvages up. Pin the edges down. Lay the pattern pieces out onto the wrong side of the fabrics. The back, the front, and the collar facing pieces go on the ecru fabric; the sleeve pieces go on the red fabric.

Position the center of the back piece over the fabric fold line. Pin the patterns to the fabric. Trace along the edges of all the pieces and take down matching marks as well. Cut the fabric pieces out by following the trace marks.

Child's cardigan age 4T

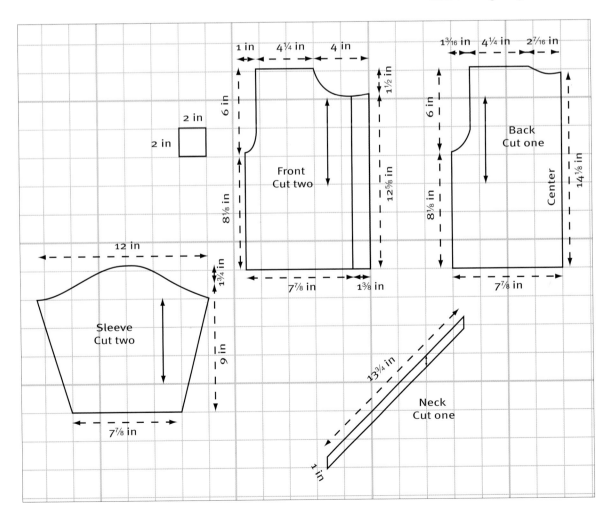

THE CHILD'S JACKET
IN 6 STEPS

Fleece is a soft, thick fabric that is easy to work with. But you should still follow these steps carefully to achieve satisfying results.

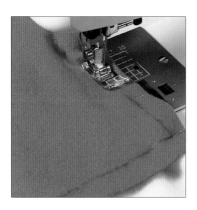

1 PREPARING THE FRONT FACINGS

Run a basting thread in a contrasting color along the fold lines in the facings for each of the two front sides (see the pattern on page 174).

With right sides together and without using too much force, use an iron to create a gentle fold on each of these facings for each side of the cardigan. Then baste the folds.

2 PREPARING THE COLLAR FACING

With the right sides together, place the two front fabric pieces on top of the back piece. Pin the shoulders together and stitch ⅝ inch from the edges.

Using an iron, press a lengthwise fold in the collar facing. Position the facing along the neckline. Make sure that the assembly markings coincide. Pin and baste.

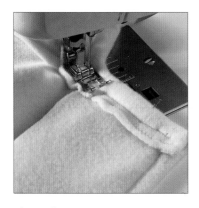

3 ATTACHING THE COLLAR FACING

You can sew the collar facing in two stages. Begin with the center back fabric piece and work toward first one front edge and then the other. Stitch within ⅜ inch of the edge. Position the ends of the collar facing so that they are under the front facings. Clip the seam allowances.

Turn the collar facing inward using an iron. Topstitch ¼ inch from the edge, making sure that you stitch through all the layers.

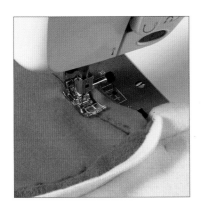

4 JOINING THE SLEEVES

Fold the sleeves in half with right sides together. Pin and stitch the underarm seam of the sleeves. Press the seams open with an iron.

Set the sleeves into the armholes, right sides. Even out the excess fabric from each sleeve around the armholes. Pin, baste, and then stitch within ⅜ inch of the edge. Notch the seam allowances.

Using the iron, turn the fabric allowances so that they run in the same direction as the sleeves.

5 MAKING THE BUTTONHOLES

With tailor's chalk, mark out positions for six buttonholes.

Set the buttonhole foot onto your sewing machine. Choose the shape that you want, then adjust the stitch width for the satin stitch.

Then slide a round button the same diameter as your novelty button into the button holder on the foot; it should automatically adjust for an appropriately sized buttonhole opening (if not, see page 171).

Press down on the pedal and let the machine create the buttonhole for you. Cut the buttonhole opening using a seam ripper.

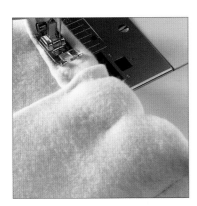

6 COMPLETING THE HEMS AND THE FRONT BANDS

Create a fold measuring 1 inch in height along the bottom of the body of the garment and at the sleeve ends using an iron. Pin and stitch ⅜ inch from the edges. Lift the facing on the bottom of the cardigan so that it can cover the hemline and conceal the stitchwork.

Place the two front fabric pieces on top and let one overlap the other by 1½ inches. Thrust a piece of tailor's chalk through each buttonhole opening and mark the locations for your buttons.

FINISHING

You can attach classic two- or four-holed plain buttons or more fanciful novelty shank buttons at these locations. Or just ask your little one for recommendations.

For more on how to position and attach the buttons, refer to the descriptions that appear on pages 156–157.

Piped Buttonholes

PRELIMINARIES

The piped buttonhole is finished with strips that are either cut from the fabric that the article is made with or from fabric that contrasts with it, depending on the effect that is desired. This kind of finishing is also used in making pockets.

Buttonholes of this sort can be tailored on all varieties of sewing machines, including those that are not capable of making zigzag stitches.

MORE ABOUT THE TECHNIQUE

The construction of the piped buttonhole involves edging and strengthening the opening using a small strip of piping. This strip, which may be square or rectangular, is first stitched onto the right side of the flap, then turned inward through the buttonhole opening before it is secured to the back of the button flap.

STEP 1

Use basting thread to mark the center of the button flap.

Then use tailor's chalk to mark the outline of the flap on the right side of your article.

STEP 2

In the fabric that you have chosen for the piping, cut out a small rectangle (or square) along the straight grain. The dimensions of this piece should be equal to those of the buttonhole opening plus an additional 1½ inches all around the perimeter.

STEP 3

Mark the outline of the buttonhole in the center of this piping rectangle. That is, inside the rectangle you just drew, draw another rectangle that is ⅛ inch smaller than the buttonhole on all sides.

STEP 4

Center the piping rectangle over the buttonhole, right sides together. Pin, then stitch along the edges of the inner rectangle.

STEP 5

Use a pair of narrow scissors to cut through the center of each buttonhole. Stop cutting when you are $\frac{1}{8}$ inch from each end and cut these ends diagonally to each corner.

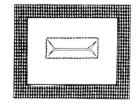

STEP 6

Slide the piece of piping fabric through the buttonhole opening and turn it down onto the wrong side of the article. On the right side you should see lips of fabric edging the buttonhole opening.

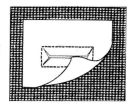

STEP 7

On the wrong side of the small fabric rectangle, create two folds of the piping fabric, making one fold from each side of the opening, so that the folded edges lie parallel to the buttonhole opening. Check that the depths of the folds are equal and meet at the exact center of the opening.

   Press the folds with the iron and baste along these folded edges. Secure the ends of the folds with two backstitches (see diagram).

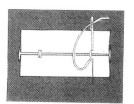

STEP 8

Hold the fabric and piping layers together and topstitch the edge on the right side of your work.

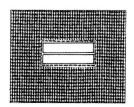

ON THE SEWING MACHINE

To produce even seams in Steps 4 and 8 above, set the sewing machine on "slow" and make small stitches that are each $\frac{1}{16}$ inch in length.

   Count the number of stitches that you make along the first edge of the buttonhole that you work on so that you can complete the same number of stitches along the other edge. Work patiently to ensure the best results for your project.

The Seat Cushion

A seat cushion is the best solution to chairs that are a bit hard to sit on. And if you select fabrics that match the decor of your room, it will only serve to make your interior a little more "you." These cushions are especially welcome on garden chairs. They are convenient because they can be easily put away in inclement weather or removed for routine cleaning.

YOU WILL NEED

(for one cushion)
Cotton pique, 1 yard by 44–45 inches wide, in yellow
Scraps of cotton fabric, in orange, red and fuchsia
Cotton cording, 32 inches by 1³⁄₁₆ inches diameter, in a color that matches the main fabric of the cushion
Foam cushion, 16 inches per side and ¾ inch thick; the two front corners should be rounded
Sewing thread, in yellow
Fine pins
Three large flat buttons, 1 inch in diameter each
Plastic triangle
Yardstick
Tailor's chalk
Narrow scissors
Dressmaker's scissors

MEASUREMENTS
Measure the length and width of the seats of your chairs and stools.

Cut out pieces of ¾-inch thick foam cushion to fit these dimensions.

FABRIC DIMENSIONS
The seat cushion shown in the photograph on the opposite page measures 16 inches on each side and is ¾ inch thick. You should add ⅝ inch all around as seam allowances.

Also make sure that you allow enough fabric for the two strips that will be used as the gussets for the cushion (see the pattern on page 182).

CHOOSING A FABRIC
For these kinds of everyday items, it is really important that you use a sturdy fabric that does not crease. Give preference to cotton fabrics, deckchair-type fabrics, ticking, or cretonne.

All of these fabrics can be easily washed by machine.

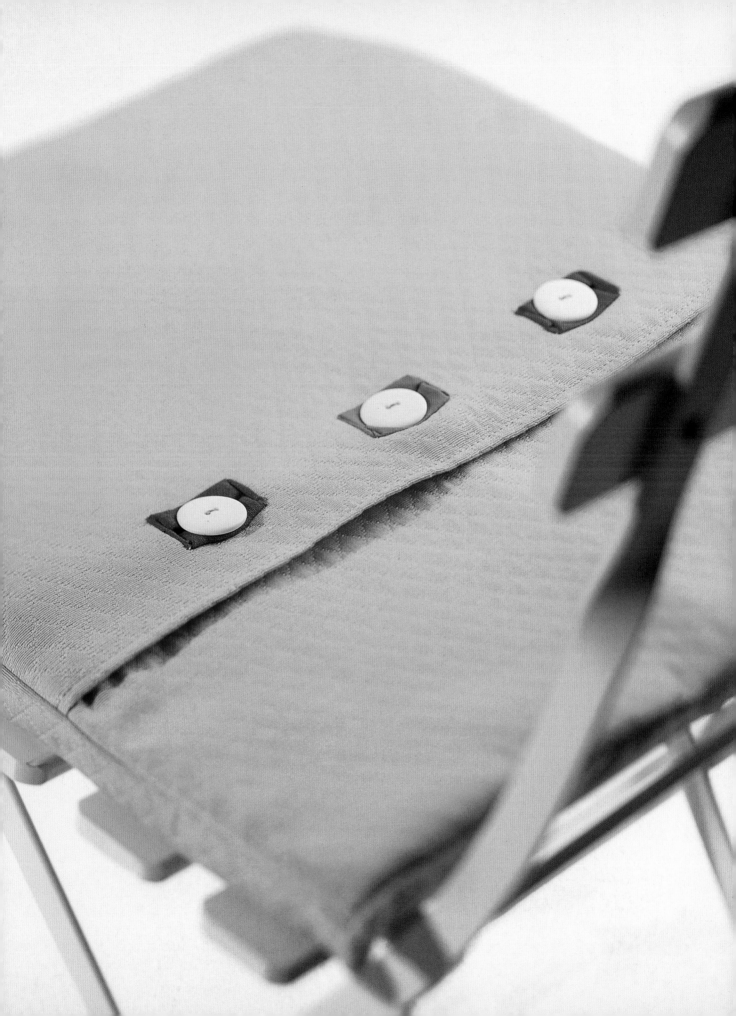

For the cushion covering, the scraps and the cotton braiding, select fabrics whose colors go well with the decor of your room. Even if your cushions are primarily there to be sat upon, your choice of colors and the finishing touches you add can easily make or break your design scheme. Give some thought to some of these details before you start.

CUTTING THE FABRIC

On the wrong side of the yellow cotton pique, use the piece of tailor's chalk, the yardstick, and the plastic triangle to trace the outlines of the three pieces of fabric for the cushion covers. These should include the bottom piece, two half-top pieces (they should differ in shape only on the corners) and the two rectangles that will be used for the gusset. Cut out the fabric pieces ⅝ inch from the trace marks.

From the cotton scraps that are in different but coordinating colors, cut out three squares that measure 4⅛ inches per side. These squares will be used to make piping for the buttonholes and thus will be partially visible on the right side of the completed cushion. Choose your colors carefully even though these are just fabric scraps.

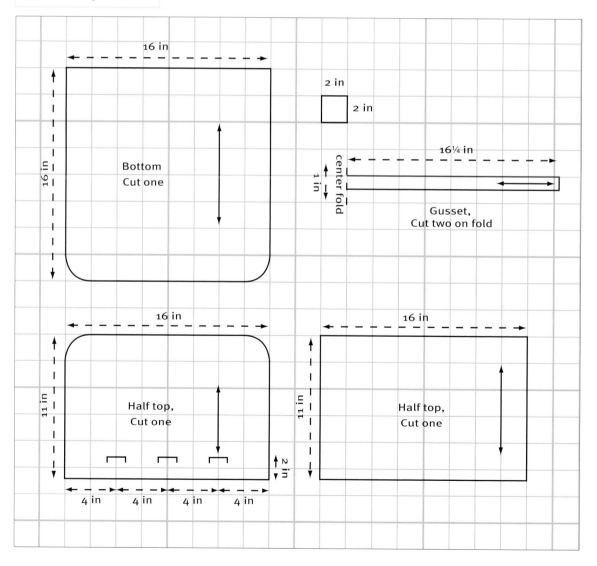

THE SEAT CUSHION
IN 4 STEPS

Overcast all of the cotton pique fabric pieces before you start putting the seat cushion together.
Follow the steps below in order.

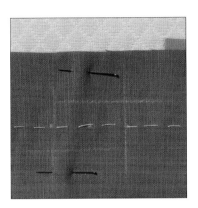

1 PREPARING THE THREE BUTTONHOLES

Use a piece of tailor's chalk to mark out the sites for the three buttonholes on the top fabric piece that has the two rounded corners (see the pattern on page 182).

The centers of the buttonholes should be 2 inches distant from the edge. Using basting thread, baste these points for later reference.

With the right sides together, pin the center of each cotton square on the thread markings for the buttonholes.

2 COMPLETING THE EDGES OF THE BUTTONHOLE

Pin, baste, and then slowly stitch along the outlines of the rectangle at the center of each colored square using a 1/16-inch stitch length.

Make sure that the stitches are parallel to each other and to the line that marks the unopened buttonhole opening. These three cotton squares, which will be used for piping, are primarily what makes this cushion unique. Give them the attention that they deserve.

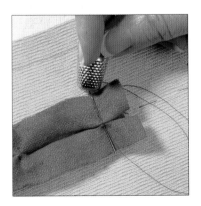

3 MAKING THE PIPING

Use a pair of narrow scissors (or the sharp end of a seam ripper) to cut through the center of each buttonhole. Then cut the ends to the corners. Push the fabric through the buttonhole openings to create the piped "lips."

On the wrong side of the fabric, set the folds using an iron and secure the ends of the buttonholes using two backstitches each.

On the right side of your work, hold the main fabric and the colored piping layers together and topstitch the edge.

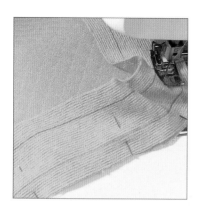

ASSEMBLING THE CASE

Fold under ⅝ inch along straight center edge of each half-top fabric piece. Pin and stitch ⅜ inch from folded edge. With right sides facing up, place the sewn edge of the buttonhole piece over the sewn edge of the second top piece to form a unit 16 inches long. Baste the overlapping side edges.

Join the gusset strips, adjusting length as needed to fit the perimeter of the bottom piece and the top unit. (To allow for adjustments, trim off any excess fabric only after seaming is completed.) Pin the gusset to the top, with the right sides together. Stitch ⅝ inch in from the edge. Notch the corners.

FINISHING

Press open the seams with an iron. Turn the case inside out through the opening. Cut the cotton cord into two pieces.

Attach the center of each piece of cord to the back of the gusset by hand, one at each back corner. Tie the ends to the back of the chair to keep the cushion in place.

All you have left to do is to mark the locations for the buttons using a piece of chalk through each of the three buttonholes, to sew the buttons on, to insert the foam cushion into the case, and finally, to button it up.

6

WORKING WITH SPECIAL FABRICS

Coated Fabrics

PRELIMINARIES

Whether you are dealing with oilcloth or rubberized, vinyl-coated, or plasticized fabrics like PVC, coated fabrics are found everywhere. They are used on decorative articles as well as wearable items such as raincoats.

Because their surfaces have been treated, these fabrics do not glide so easily through or between the presser foot and the feed dogs of your sewing machine. But there are efficient methods for working with them so long as you have the necessary accessories. Furthermore, these fabrics have a very desirable quality: They do not fray.

MORE ABOUT THE TECHNIQUE

Coated fabrics belong to the group of fabrics called technical fabrics. These are fabrics that do not have visible warps and wefts, or at the very least have wefts that are not woven but knitted. To achieve success with these kinds of materials, you have to become familiar with their unique features.

STEP 1

Set a nonstick (Teflon) foot onto your sewing machine. This foot generally does not come with the original sewing machine purchase, but all the major manufacturers should sell it. Since this supplemental accessory is very useful, you should make sure to buy one in advance.

STEP 2

Insert a fine needle (size 70 or 80) into your machine. You want to use a new needle so that the point can penetrate the fabric easily without any chance of tearing.

STEP 3

Load polyester thread onto the bobbin pins. This thread is very strong but still flexible enough to give seams a sufficient amount of elasticity.

STEP 4

Prepare the machine for a straight stitch with a length of at least ⅛ inch. The stitches should be long enough to prevent the surface of the fabric from being damaged. If your stitches are too small, you risk crumpling the fabric.

STEP 5

Coated fabrics cannot be sewn using the same pins or the basting stitches that you usually use with other fabrics since the holes that these leave are unfortunately all too visible.

Use masking tape to keep the pieces in place as you work. Remove all the tape when you are done.

STEP 6

Always work your fabric with the coated surface up against the sole of the presser foot on the sewing machine.

ON THE SEWING MACHINE

There are a number of specific presser feet like the nonstick foot that exist to make these kinds of special fabrics easier to work with.

Work slowly to ensure that the stitches are properly finished. If the stitch speed is too fast, the machine can miss stitches and leave you with unsightly seams.

The Vinyl Carrier Bag

The vinyl carrier bag is practical, durable, and will always be in fashion. It can be made in a number of colors and adapted in a lot of different ways. The model you see here is the crocodile version. Its reddish-brown tone should go well with a lot of other differently colored items. But this color is only one amid a myriad of possibilities.

YOU WILL NEED

Vinyl-coated imitation crocodile fabric, ¾ yard in by 60 inches wide, in burgundy

Thick iron-on or fusible interfacing, ⅝ inch by 45 inches wide, in white

Sewing thread, in red

Two press studs

Wide masking tape

Felt-tip pen with an extra-sharp point

Plastic triangle

Yardstick

Pinking shears

Dressmaker's scissors

MEASUREMENTS

The completed bag measures 16 inches in width by 11½ inches in height by 5½ inches in breadth.

You can modify these measurements depending upon how you plan on using your bag.

The pattern (page 190) includes seam allowances.

THE INTERFACING

It is usually possible to press coated fabrics, like vinyl, on their wrong sides. This is especially true when the coating is attached to a cloth or a knitted backing.

Nevertheless, you should always test it out on a scrap of the fabric before you actually start applying the fusible interfacing.

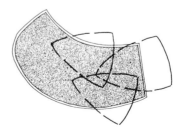

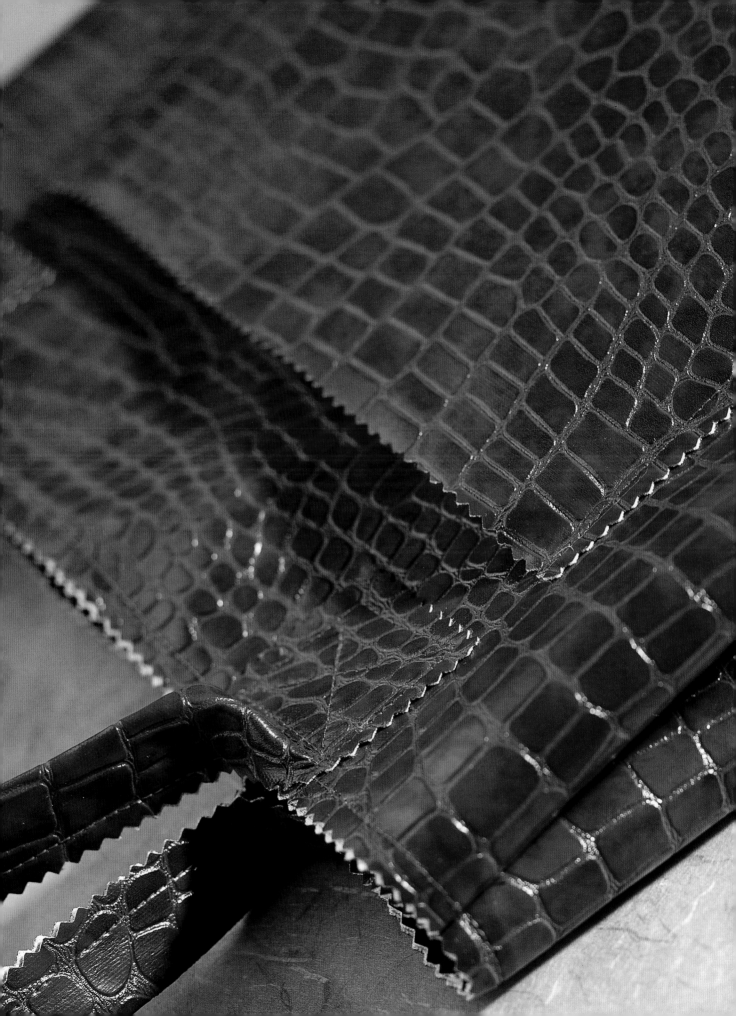

If the material that you have chosen to use on the bag cannot be pressed, you should omit applying the interfacing and move directly onto the steps that follow.

CUTTING THE FABRIC

Use the yardstick and the felt-tip pen to transfer the outlines of the pattern pieces for the bag onto the wrong side of the coated fabric. Cut along the outlines of the pieces with the pinking shears. From scraps, cut two strips 22⅞ inches by about 3 inches wide for facings.

If you have tested the fabric and it can withstand ironing, then trace the same pattern pieces onto the fusible interfacing. Use a pair of dressmaker's scissors to cut out the pieces 1/16 inch within the pattern outlines.

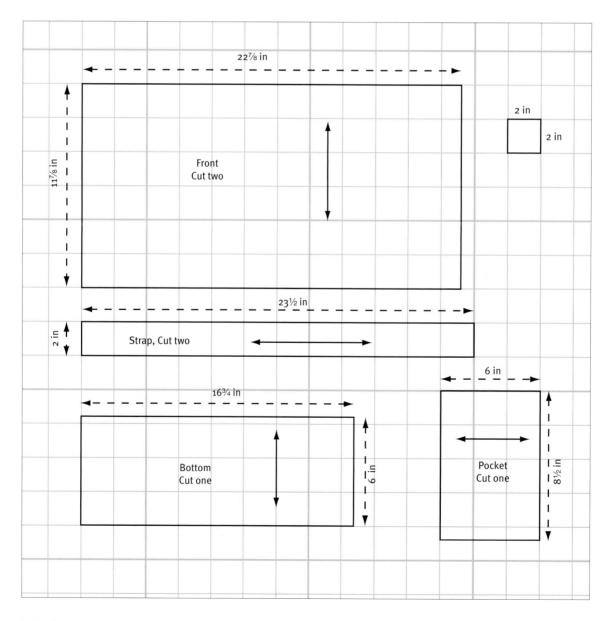

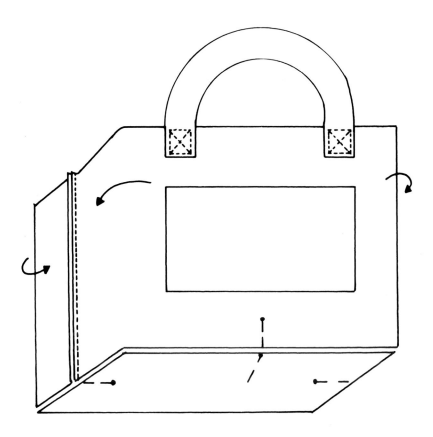

ASSEMBLY

The front sides of the bag are joined to each other end to end and can collapse inward, thus accounting for its large carrying capacity. If you want to reduce or increase the dimensions of the bag, you should particularly take note of this feature.

Therefore, once you have decided upon the width of the finished bag, extend each end of the front fabric piece by half the breadth, or simply, extend each front fabric piece by one full breadth. When the bag has been assembled (see the diagram above), the ends of each front strip are joined to their counterparts on the sides of the bag at a point that lies directly above the centerline of the bottom piece.

This type of assembly obviates the need for separate gussets and also saves you a bit of fabric when cutting the pattern. This technique is especially useful when you are working with fabrics that are somewhat more expensive like double-faced vinyl or leather. It also means that you will not have to sew so many structural seams, which are not always easy to complete in materials like imitation fur or raffia matting.

THE VINYL CARRIER BAG
IN 6 STEPS

When you have finished cutting and are ready to assemble the bag, adjust the temperature setting on your iron to silk and apply the fusible interfacing to the wrong side of each fabric piece.

1 APPLYING THE VINYL FACINGS

With wrong sides of the fabrics together, lay a strip of facing onto the wrong side along the top of one of the front pieces.

Stitch ⅜ inch from the edge.

Use the same technique to apply a strip of facing to the other front piece of the bag.

2 SEWING THE FRONT POCKET

Center the pocket on one of the front pieces and keep it in place using a few pieces of masking tape.

Complete as even a stitch as you can ¼ inch from the side and bottom edges of the pocket. Stitches that are completely straight and parallel to the serrated edges of the bag are especially important in projects like this.

3 PREPARING AND MAKING THE STRAPS

On one front section, position the ends of a strap 6⅝ inches in from each side edge and down 2 inches from the top edge. Tape ends in place.

Stitch a square whose sides are ¼ inch in from the strap edges, then complete with an X within the square. Proceed in the same way for the other strap on the remaining front. These measures will give durability to the completed bag.

COMPLETING THE STRAPS

Fold the center section of one strap in half lengthwise. Holding the serrated (pinked) edges together, stitch the edges ¼ inch from the edge, starting and ending as close to the attached ends as you can work (see photograph).

Proceed in the same way for the other strap. These measures will give durability to the completed bag.

ATTACHING THE TWO FRONT PIECES TO THE BOTTOM PIECE OF THE BAG

Use the felt-tip pen to mark the midpoints on each edge of the bottom piece. With wrong sides together, attach the bottom to the front pattern pieces of the bag, matching midpoints. Hold the pieces in place with masking tape and stitch ⅜ inch in from the edge, working from the center toward the corners.

COMPLETING THE SIDES AND FORMING THE BAG

Tape the ends of the two front fabric pieces to the two shorter sides of the bottom piece. Stitch ⅜ inch from the edge, continuing the stitching line from the corner to the midpoint of the side.

Attach the ends of the fronts together along their edges to close each side of the bag, adjusting ends to meet smoothly and trimming off excess, if needed, to make ⅜-inch seam allowances.

FINISHING

Attach press studs on the top of the left and right sides of the bag to keep the gusset in place.

This closure will add a touch of elegance to your bag and keep your documents safe from prying eyes.

Knitted Fabrics

PRELIMINARIES

In professional sewing, knitted fabrics are worked on special machines known as overlock machines or sergers. These devices make it possible to stitch and overcast hems in one shot. The seams that are finished in this manner are flexible, and cut edges, which otherwise tend to unravel so easily, retain their shape when worked on such machines.

Sewing machine manufacturers usually sell models of overlock machines that are designed for in-home use. With these machines, you can obtain results similar to those produced by machines in industry. Traditional sewing machines also offer the capability of completing stitches that can look quite professional.

MORE ABOUT THE TECHNIQUE

Knitted fabrics have a looped surface that is more or less fine and fragile. Their uniqueness lies in their supple (as with plain jersey knits or interlock – double knits) and sometimes tight-fitting (as with rib knits) quality. Also in this fabric family are stretch fabrics, whose usage in clothing is very much in vogue these days.

STEP 1

Lay one of the two pieces you want to join together on top of the other one, right sides together and matching edges. Pin, using extra-fine pins all around and spaced out 1 inch apart.

STEP 2

Adjust the sewing machine for the elastic stitch. This stitch is known for its supple results. Stitch, letting the fabric glide past the presser foot naturally.

Then recut the seam allowances ⅛ inch from the seam. When you use the elastic stitch, you do not have to overcast the seam allowances.

If your sewing machine does not have an elastic stitch feature, complete the assembly using a zigzag stitch set to a width of $\frac{1}{32}$ inch and a length of $\frac{1}{16}$ inch. As you work, stretch out the fabric using smooth movements to ensure that the seam does not gather up.

STEP 3

Load polyester thread into the bobbin. This kind of thread produces flexible seams which are indispensable for this type of work.

STEP 4

Choose a new, fine gilt point jersey needle (size 65 or 70). Some manufacturers offer needles especially made for knit fabrics.

Replace the needle often, since synthetic fabrics blunt the point quite quickly.

STEP 5

Overcast the seam allowances to ensure that they do not roll up.

Prepare the sewing machine for a zigzag stitch with a width of $\frac{1}{8}$ inch and a length of about $\frac{1}{4}$ inch.

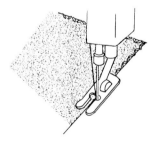

ON THE SEWING MACHINE

If your sewing machine allows you to insert a needle from the left-hand side, take advantage of this feature when completing Step 4 above.

A needle in this position makes it easier for the machine's feed dogs to hang onto the fabric, meaning that your efforts will go all the more smoothly and produce even results.

195

The Jersey Shawl

The process of assembling this shawl – or throw or blanket, if you so desire – should leave you with a greater feel for working with knitted fabrics. These fabrics are really quite ideal for your cushion covers, straight skirts, vests, blankets or cases meant for all kinds of situations.

YOU WILL NEED

Jersey, 1¼ yards by 54 inches wide, in light green

Jersey, 1⅛ yards by 54 inches wide, in prairie green

Polyester thread, 1 bobbin in prairie green

Fine pins

Yardstick

Tailor's chalk

Dressmaker's scissors

HELPFUL HINTS

You can finish a hand-knit or hand-crocheted piece on the sewing machine. The assembly is really quite straightforward. You will also find that a piece finished by machine can appear very professionally done.

MEASUREMENTS

The completed shawl is square in shape; it measures 49 inches by 49 inches of which almost 4 inches is the border.

These measurements and the shape can be easily changed if you want it so: The same principles and the same technique can be used with any rectangular piece of fabric.

CUTTING THE FABRIC

On the wrong side of the light green fabric, use tailor's chalk to mark a square measuring 42¾ inches on a side.

On the wrong side of the prairie green fabric, mark four strips, each measuring 52¾ inches in length by 8 inches in width.

Then cut out all the fabric pieces, following the trace marks.

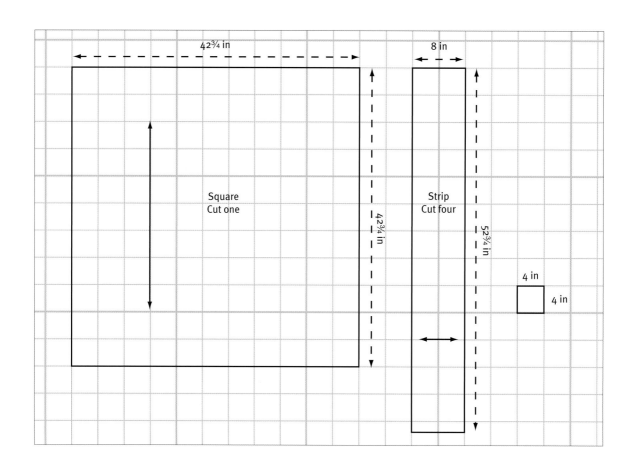

42¾ in

8 in

Square
Cut one

Strip
Cut four

42¾ in

52¾ in

4 in

4 in

THE JERSEY SHAWL
IN 4 STEPS

Once the pattern pieces have been cut out, fold each of the four prairie green strips in half lengthwise to measure 4 inches in width. Then continue with the following steps.

1 JOINING THE FIRST STRIP

With right sides together, pin one edge of the strip along a side of the large square, with the ends extending 5 inches on each side. Then elastic stitch the seam ⅜ inch in from the inner edge.

Fold under the edge of the second half of the strip to create a ⅜-inch hem fold and stitch this fold in place while holding onto the edge of the square.

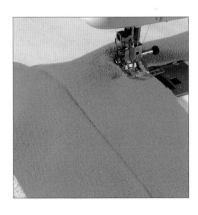

LAYING DOWN THE OTHER STRIPS SEQUENTIALLY FROM THE FIRST ONE

Pin the three remaining strips that you have cut out and prepared, then join them to the square one by one, exactly in the same way that you did for the first (see Step 1).

Each strip you add on should overlap over the previous one. Work around the entire shawl in this manner. You will be completing the corners a little bit later.

WORKING THE CORNERS

At each corner, trim back the end of the underlying strip by 3⅛ inches to reduce bulk and slide it under the adjacent strip. Pin it carefully so that all fabric layers remain in place.

On the end of the outer untrimmed strip, use an iron to fold in ends to make this edge even with the adjacent strip. Pin this fold.

TOPSTITCHING THE HEMS

Stitch the side of each strip ¼ inch in from the edge to maintain the hems.

To do this, leave the needle in the fabric at one of the corners. Lift the presser foot of the sewing machine and pivot the fabric 45 degrees (see how the right-angled corner is done on page 56).

At ¼ inch in from the edge, complete a stitch along the part of the strip that is concealed by its neighbor.

FINISHING

At the end you can add finishing touches to the topstitching.

Depending on what you are going to use the shawl for and depending upon your taste, you can apply a colored ribbon, a braid, or a fringed strip to the edges of the shawl or even directly to the topstitched seams.

Let your imagination run wild.

Velvet Fabrics

PRELIMINARIES

Although it is delicate to work with and tends to retain creases that are hard to eliminate, velvet is nevertheless a beautiful material.

Several kinds of velvet exist: silk velvet, cotton velvet, and woolen velvet for home furnishings, among others. The more elegant varieties of velvet including crushed, embossed, and panne velvets, each of which is as lustrous as the others, can greatly enrich even the most basic of your projects.

MORE ABOUT THE TECHNIQUE

Unlike other technical fabrics, velvet fabrics, even if they do not have visible weft, nevertheless have direction. You must take note of this when you cut out the pattern pieces. Before you do anything else, make sure that you always know the fabric direction.

STEP 1

To determine the direction of the velvet, pass the flat of your hand over the surface pile. If the velvet shimmers, the pile is running down. If the color of the velvet intensifies and your hand leaves a impression on the fabric, the pile is running up.

Choose one direction or the other and set your pattern pieces along the straight grain of the chosen direction.

STEP 2

Install an even-feed or roller foot into your sewing machine. A nonstick foot is also appropriate for this project.

These kinds of presser feet make your work easier by ensuring that the two pieces of fabric do not separate from each other during assembly.

STEP 3

Insert fine pins all around and spaced 1¼ inches apart. They should be perpendicular to the edges of the pieces being assembled.

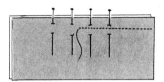

STEP 4

The thickness of the needle you use with your machine will depend upon the thickness of the velvet.

For thicker velvets, use a size 70 needle.

For velvets intended for home furnishings, use a size 90 or even a size 100 needle.

If you do make a mistake during assembly, undo the stitchwork using a seam ripper.

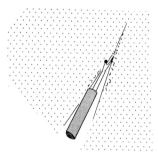

ON THE SEWING MACHINE

Even if you do not have to push or pull the velvet through the sewing machine yourself, you should still maintain a firm grip over it. To do so, lay your hands out flat on both sides of the presser foot, as close to the needle as you can get.

Reduce the pressure of the presser foot so that it does not leave a mark on the surface of the velvet. Try the machine out a few times on fabric scraps before you actually begin assembly.

The Vest

This vest is extremely simple in design and does not require a lining. You can use as many kinds of velvet in as many colors as you wish with this garment. The only rule is that you should make sure that you cut your pattern pieces in the same direction as the fabric, as with all other works that involve velvet.

YOU WILL NEED

Synthetic velvet, $7/8$ yard by 54 inches wide, in russet

Polyester thread, in russet

Fine pins

Yardstick

Tailor's chalk

Dressmaker's scissors

HELPFUL HINTS

This long and modest vest is especially suited to an adult. However, you can also reduce the dimensions of the pattern pieces so that it can fit a child or a teenager. If you use high-quality velvet, the vest can be worn on special occasions.

MEASUREMENTS

Take the bust and hip measurements (see page 247) of the individual who is to wear this vest.

Then take the length from the shoulder to the hips and the length from the base of the nape to the hips.

Adjust the pattern according to the measurements you obtain.

FABRIC DIMENSIONS

For fabric that measures 44–45 inches or 54 inches in width, you need a length of fabric equal to the height of the vest plus any seam allowances. For larger sizes, double this amount for 44–45 inches width fabrics.

CUTTING THE FABRIC

The figures for the hem ($1^{3}/_{16}$ inches) and for the seam allowances ($5/8$ inch) are already included in the pattern measurements. Fold the fabric in half and lay out a front pattern piece and a piece of front facing onto its wrong side; make sure that all pieces are in line with the straight grain and the pile direction. Position the center of the back pattern piece over the fabric fold line.

Use the tailor's chalk to trace the outlines of the pattern pieces and cut out the fabric pieces by following the trace marks (see the pattern on page 204).

size 14 vest

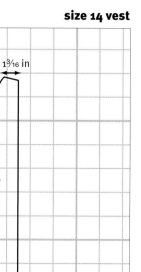

2 in 4¾ in 3½ in 1¾ in 3½ in 3 in 1³⁄₁₆ in

1 in

9½ in

Back
Cut on fold

9¼ in

9¼ in

9¼ in

Center fold

Front
Cut two

Front facing

16½ in

17¾ in

16½ in

17¾ in

Cut two

2 in

2 in

10½ in 8¼ in 3 in

THE VEST IN 4 STEPS

Even if you choose to adorn it with braids or novelty trims, the vest's simplicity of design will nevertheless remain appealing. Overcast the fabric pieces before you begin assembly.

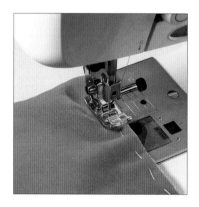

1 THE NECKLINE AND ARMHOLE HEM FOLDS

For the back piece, fold under ⅝ inch along the neckline edge. Pin, then baste. Topstitch ¼ inch from the fold. With right sides together, lay the two front pieces over the back. Pin shoulder edges together and seam.

Fold under ⅝ inch around each armhole, rounding and evening out the cap portion of the fold. Pin, baste, and topstitch.

If you prefer, use single-fold bias tape (see page 223) to face these curved edges, trimming fabric seam allowance to slightly less than ¼ inch.

2 ATTACHING THE FRONT FACINGS

With right sides together, lay the facings on top of the two front pieces. Pin the front edges together then stitch.

Trim the seam allowances to within ¼ inch of the seam and turn the facings toward the inside of the vest.

Use a slipstitch to hand-sew the top of each facing to the vest beneath the shoulder seam allowances.

3 ATTACHING THE TWO FRONTS TO THE BACK PIECE

Here you use a well-known technique for joining three separate pieces.

With right sides together, pin the two sides of the vest to each other and stitch carefully.

Before you start working on the bottom hem, press the seams open. It is easier to flatten the seams at this juncture; the hem you make will also be neater.

4 MAKING THE BOTTOM HEM OF THE VEST

Use the iron to press a ⅜-inch fold along the entire vest bottom. Pin the fold in place. Form a second ¾-inch fold over the first by hand.

Sew in this second fold by hand using a hem stitch to achieve a more supple finish and a more natural drape. Topstitch the neckline and the armholes ¼ inch in from the edge.

FINISHING

This finishing touch is optional. Pin a novelty trim or braid onto the vest fronts ¾ inch in from the edges.

Sew on the trim or braid by hand using a slipstitch so that it will go perfectly with the drape of the vest.

Imitation Fur Fabrics

PRELIMINARIES

Imitation fur is available in a variety of textures and colors. Woven from either long or short hairs, fur fabrics may imitate the natural coat of the panther, the leopard, the mink, or some other animal or they may be printed with a whimsical motif. These fabrics may be used to create all sorts of items, big or small.

These items range widely from plush toys for the newborn infant to comfortable winter coats and from blankets to sofa cushions; the choice is yours to make.

MORE ABOUT THE TECHNIQUE

Like velvet fabrics, imitation fur fabrics have direction. Therefore, you need to figure out the fabric direction and make a note of it prior to tracing and cutting out the fabric pieces; you do not want to finish your work only to find out that you made a mistake here.

STEP 1

When tracing the outlines of the pattern pieces onto the wrong side of the imitation fur fabric, make sure that all the pieces are oriented in the same direction. Follow the straight grain indicator.

To determine the direction of the hairs, pass your hand over the fabric: If the hairs stay down and the surface shimmers, you have found the natural direction of the pile. If the hairs spring back up and the fur takes on a darker tone, the direction of the pile runs in the opposite direction.

STEP 2

When you lay one piece of imitation fur fabric over another with the intent of joining them, place the fur-lined sides together and push the hairs at the edge into your item so that they do not get caught up in the seam.

STEP 3

Use extra-fine steel pins and stick them in perpendicular to the edge of the fabric. Position them closely together, spaced about 1 inch apart, to prevent the pieces from sliding when you work them later on the machine.

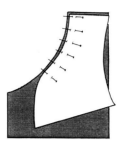

STEP 4

Prepare the sewing machine for a straight stitch with a length of ⅛ inch. Install a size 90 needle.

STEP 5

Stitch on the wrong side of the imitation fur. Use a pin to push hairs that are caught in the seam back out onto the right side of the piece.

STEP 6

Trim the excess fabric to within ⅛ inch of the edge of the seams to slim down the assembly.

ON THE SEWING MACHINE

To assemble items using imitation fur fabrics, you must adjust the pressure of the presser foot so that it is suitable for working items of this thickness. Reduce the pressure by a notch or two to keep the fabric from becoming caught in the machine.

Always try out your technique on a sample before working on the actual item.

The Stuffed Teddy Bear

Stuffed toys are projects that require delicate cutting and assembly. But what joy they can bring once they are finished! Today's fabric shops offer an extended range of imitation furs – short hair, long hair, different designs, different colors; really, anything goes. For toys intended for young children, you must select a fabric that is short-haired and machine-washable.

MEASUREMENTS
The stuffed teddy bear in the photograph on the opposite page is about 10 inches tall when seated.

The pattern for this model can be easily enlarged or reduced using a photocopier.

FABRIC DIMENSIONS
Imitation fur is sold in widths of 60 inches.

For a stuffed bear of this size, ⅝ yard should be ample; you might even be able to use the scraps to make one or two tinier teddy bears.

CUTTING THE FABRIC
The double-headed arrow that appears on each pattern piece indicates the straight grain and the direction of the imitation fur fabric. Arrange the pattern pieces so that the hairs are always oriented in the same direction. Fold the fabric in half with right sides together.

Position and pin on the pattern pieces labeled A, B, C, F, G, H, and I. Use the felt-tip pen to trace the edges of the patterns and the numbered markings onto the fabric. Cut out the pieces along the trace marks.

Unfold the fabric and cut out pieces D and E.

On the scrap of pink cotton, trace two pieces each for A and J. Cut these pieces ⅜ inch beyond the trace marks.

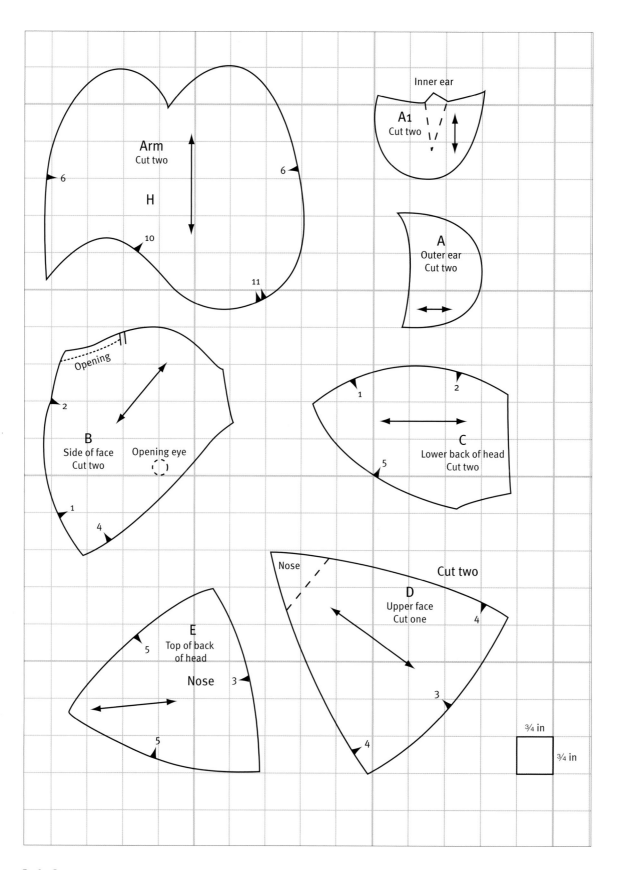

Inner ear

A1
Cut two

A
Outer ear
Cut two

Arm
Cut two

H

6   6

10

11

Opening

2

B
Side of face
Cut two

Opening eye

1   2

5

C
Lower back of head
Cut two

1

4

Nose

Cut two

D
Upper face
Cut one

4

3

E
Top of back
of head

5

Nose   3

4

5

¾ in

¾ in

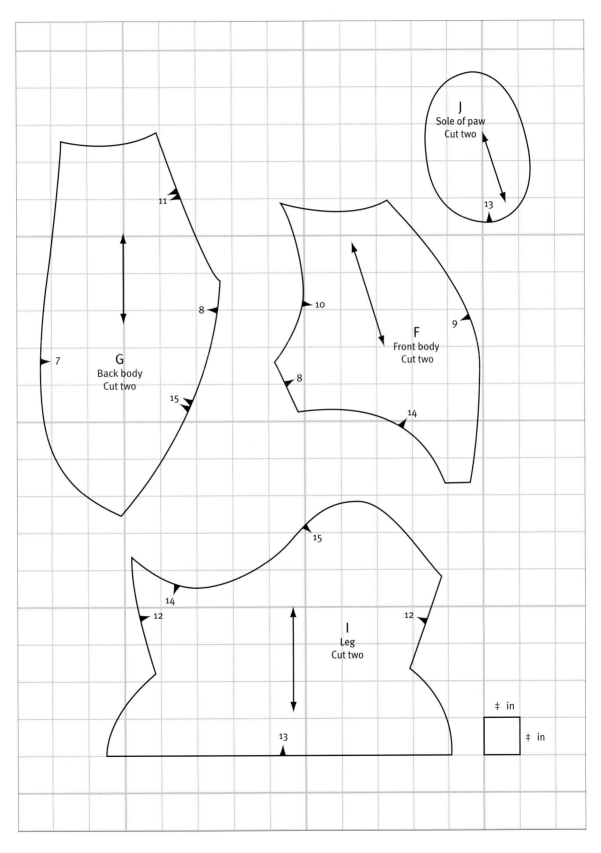

J
Sole of paw
Cut two
13

11

7

8

G
Back body
Cut two

15

10

9

F
Front body
Cut two

8

14

15

14

12

12

I
Leg
Cut two

13

‡ in

‡ in

EMBROIDERING

Choose your materials wisely since this item is for small children. Just as you chose the short-haired fabric for reasons of hygiene and cleanliness, avoid using buttons for the eyes of the bear.

Only use buttons with bears that are solely decorative or that are meant for older children. However, for this model simply embroider the eyes and the nose using a thread in a contrasting color.

THE STUFFED TEDDY BEAR
IN 6
STEPS

Make sure that you have precisely transferred the locations of markings 1 to 15 onto pattern pieces A to J of the pattern. They will be indispensable when it comes time to assemble all the pieces.

1 MOUNTING THE EARS

Pin the darts on the back of the two A1 pieces, then stitch them.

With the right sides together, join A pieces to the A1 pieces around the curved edges. Turn each ear right side out. Add a little stuffing to each and with a zigzag stitch, close the bottom. Attach the outer edge of and the ear to each B piece at marking 1, with the pink side turned toward the front of the head. The ears will be sewn in straddling pieces B and D.

2 EMBROIDERING THE EYES AND THE NOSE

Begin by embroidering the eyes using a satin stitch onto each of the B pieces (sides of face). Then embroider the nose, again using a satin stitch, onto piece D (upper face). With right sides of the fabric together, join the B pieces to the C pieces (lower back of head) by lining up markings 1 and 2, then join piece D to the B pieces by lining up the 4 markings, attaching the bottom shapes of the ear in seam.

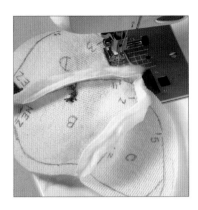

COMPLETING THE HEAD

By now, the two ears should be attached to the head of the teddy bear (see Step 1 and 2).

Sew piece E (top of back of head) to the C pieces (lower back of head) by lining up the 5 markings and to piece D (upper face) by aligning the 3 markings (see the pattern pieces for the head on page 210).

Close off the bottom of the nose by joining the B pieces (sides of face) to each other up to the parallel line marking. Turn the head of the teddy bear right side out.

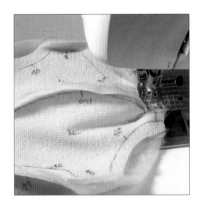

COMPLETING THE BODY

Align the 9 markings, then stitch the F pieces (front body) together. Sew together the G pieces (back body) from the 7 marks down to the end of the rounded area. Join pieces F and G along the side seams below the arm opening by lining up the 8 marks (see pattern); center seams of each section are aligned. Leaving leg openings, sew together the crotch following the contours of the F pieces. Hand-baste the tips of the F and G pieces together at each shoulder, leaving arm and neck openings.

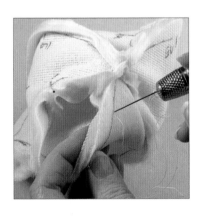

COMPLETING THE ARMS AND THE LEGS

Fold one H piece (arm) to line up the 6 marks, then stitch edges, leaving an opening between marks 10 and 11. Repeat on the other H piece. Turn the arms right side out. Set them partially into the interior of the body at the arm openings, lining up marks 10 and 11 of each unit, stitch together by hand using a backstitch.

By hand, using a backstitch, seam each I (leg) piece along the edges with the 12 marks. Aligning the 13 marks, join a J piece (sole) to each leg. Turn legs right side out. Set one leg partially into a leg opening on the body, matching 14 and 15 marks. Sew edges together by hand. Repeat for the other leg and opening.

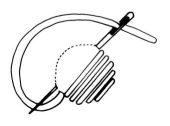

Satin stitch for embroidering the nose of the teddy bear

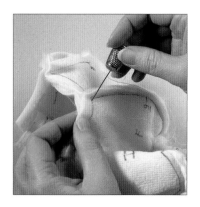

6 JOINING THE HEAD TO THE BODY OF THE TEDDY BEAR

Set the head onto the body of the teddy bear.

Attach the head and body by hand with backstitches, joining the front body of the lower edge of the face and the back to the lower back of the head, leaving the center back opening for stuffing.

FINISHING

Slip the stuffing into the teddy bear. Pack it in well. Get the stuffing into the legs and the snout by gently prodding with a knitting needle.

Finish by closing the opening at the back of the head and the body with a small slipstitch. Wrap a decorative ribbon around the neck of the teddy bear and knot it any way you wish.

7

EDGINGS AND FINISHINGS, BIAS BINDING, AND PIPING

Attaching Inserts

PRELIMINARIES

An insert is a ribbon, a braid, or other fabric inserted between two strips of flat fabric. This finishing is used with bed linen, fine lingerie, and blouses. It can serve to highlight the article being made and consolidates all the elements of an article while giving it a touch of finesse, elegance, and refinement.

MORE ABOUT THE TECHNIQUE

The insert may or may not be lined depending on the thickness or the transparency of the fabrics that are used to make it. In either case, it should be made as neatly and evenly as possible. The insert can simultaneously bring suppleness and solidity to a piece.

THE UNLINED INSERT

This method is appropriate for lightweight or diaphanous fabrics where the preservation of transparency is a must.

STEP 1

Cut out the two straight pieces of fabric between which the insert will be placed. Fold the edges not bordering the insert to make a hem, folding up approximately ⅝ inch and turning under the raw edges. Baste.

Then form a ¼-inch hem along the two sides of the insert. Baste the hem.

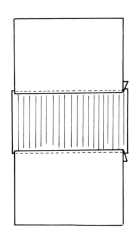

STEP 2

Pin the insert onto the edge of the first straight piece. The side hem of this piece should conceal the hem of the insert. Stitch ⅛ inch in from the edge. Make sure that you stitch through all the layers.

STEP 3

Pin the insert onto the edge of the second straight piece. The hem of this piece should conceal the opposite hem of the insert. Stitch ⅛ inch in from the edge, stitching through all the layers.

STEP 4

Stitch the basted hems on the ends of the insert. The ends of the straight pieces should align with the ends of the insert to form one continuous whole without any jogs.

THE LINED INSERT

This technique is used on thick fabrics to conceal areas that are too bulky.

STEP 1

Overcast the two strips of fabric and the insert. With right sides together, lay the edge of the first flat strip over the edge of the insert. Pin, then stitch ⅜ inch in from the edges.

STEP 2

Align the edge of the second flat strip with the other side of the insert and stitch. Press the seams open using an iron while turning the seams down toward the flat strips.

STEP 3

Place the lining over the unit, right sides together. Pin, then stitch ⅜ inch in from the edges. Leave the last 6 inches open.

STEP 4

Press the seams open with an iron while turning them toward the lining. Turn the work inside out through the opening.

Stretch the corners outward and iron the surface while directing the folds inward. Close the opening by hand using a few slipstitches.

The Silk Stole

Here is an example of how an insert can be used to harmonize two fabrics: a beautifully woven silk weave and a transparent muslin ribbon. By varying the dimensions of this color-contrasting model while applying the same technique in all cases, you can create sophisticated curtains, exotic cushion slipcovers, or multicolored table toppers.

YOU WILL NEED

Silk weave, 1 yard by 60 inches wide
Muslin ribbon, 4⅜ yards by 2⅜ inches wide
Sewing thread, in a color that matches the background color of the weave
Special machine embroidery thread No. 30, in a matching or a contrasting color
Fine pins
Dressmaker's scissors

HELPFUL HINTS

The insert requires careful working but allows for a large degree of creativity. Let your imagination run wild. Add a personal touch to an austere-looking item, or transform an ordinary piece of clothing into something much more refined.

FABRIC DIMENSIONS

For this project, you need fabric measuring 1 yard by 60 inches.

However, for this technique dimensions mostly need to be calculated on a piece-by-piece basis. Below you will find measurements for the strips that make up the surface of the stole.

CUTTING THE FABRIC

Cut two strips each measuring 18 inches by 55½ inches from the silk weave. At each end of the silk strips, remove a strip that is 4¾ inches in width and another that is 8 inches in width. You should be left with two strips that measure 18 inches by 30 inches.

Also cut out eight strips from the muslin ribbon that are each 18 inches in length.

ON THE SEWING MACHINE

When working on the insert, it might be interesting to topstitch using one of the whimsical embroidery stitches available on some modern sewing machines. However, a simple topstitch works just as well. Work on a sample to determine the proper setting for the stitch and to adapt it to the width of the insert.

Apply the fancy stitch ⅛ inch in from the edges of the flat pieces above the previous stitch and on both sides of the insert.

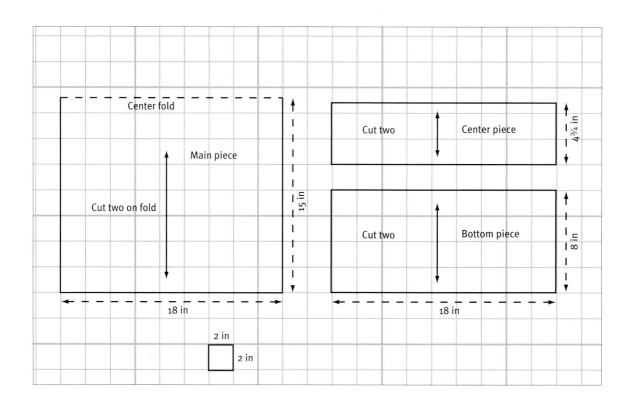

THE SILK STOLE
IN 4 STEPS

Lay out all the cut pieces flat for one last time to verify that your measurements have been exact and that the designs line up correctly. Overcast the silk strips before you start assembly.

1 APPLYING THE INSERT

With right sides together and matching 18-inch edges, place one of the edges of the muslin ribbon over one side of the 8-inch strip. Pin it in place. On the opposite side of the ribbon, place one side of the 4¾-inch strip. Pin it in place.

Place another piece of muslin ribbon over the opposite of the 4¾-inch strip. Pin it in place. Place a side of the long strip onto the opposite side of the second ribbon. Pin it in place.

2 STITCHING THE INSERTS AND PRESSING THE STRIPS

Stitch the sides that you have already assembled ¼ inch in from the edges, then join strips as for Step 1 (but in reverse order) to make the corresponding end of the stole.

Use the tip of the iron to press the seams open, then flatten the seam allowances so that they run in the same direction as the silk strips.

3 TOPSTITCHING THE STRIPS AND THE INSERT

Adjust your sewing machine to the triple stitch setting and set the stitch length to ³⁄₁₆ inch.

Fill the bobbin with the No. 30 special machine embroidery thread. Use a thread color that matches or contrasts against the background of the stole. Stitch ⅛ inch from the edge.

4 ATTACHING THE LINING

Repeat all the steps to make the second strip joining silk and inserts as before. With the right sides of the fabrics together, lay one of the two stole pieces over the other and pin the pieces together.

Stitch ⅜ inch from the edge. Leave a 6-inch opening along one of the sides. Cut the allowances once again ¼ inch from the seam. Press the seams open with an iron. Turn the piece right side out.

FINISHING

Fold the cut edges of the opening inside the stole and press. Close the opening by hand with a slip stitch.

With the wrong sides together, place one strip over the other, aligning the corresponding sections of the two strips. Pin the layers together, section by section. Topstitch the borders of the stole with the embroidery thread.

Attaching Bias Binding

PRELIMINARIES

Bias binding is a piece of tape with rectilinear edges and a straight grain that is set at 45 degrees. These qualities make it possible for you to use the binding to edge straight as well as curved shapes. It is particularly well-suited for finishing the edges of your projects. In addition, bias binding is very decorative.

It is possible to purchase precut bias binding that is sold in lengths of 3 yards. The tape should come with folded edges, which makes application easier.

MORE ABOUT THE TECHNIQUE

Whether you decide to use a prefolded bias binding or to make your own, choose a width and a color that go well with the article being edged and the composition of the supporting fabric. The ensemble should be harmonious in every respect.

MAKING BIAS BINDING

If you cannot find a bias binding in the shop that fits your needs, you can make your own out of a fabric of your own choice.

Here are a few words of advice on how to make your own bias binding.

STEP 1

Cut out a strip along the true bias of the fabric that you have selected. On the wrong side, mark out parallel lines for as many tapes as you need at a 45-degree angle to the straight grain.

The width of these tapes should always correspond to the measurement of the bias binding before you fold it.

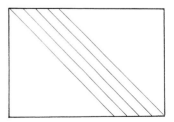

STEP 2

Place the right sides of the two straight grain ends of a strip together, each time shifting by the width of a strip.

Pin and then stitch ⅜ inch in. Press open the seams with an iron.

STEP 3

Cut the strip in one continuous motion. Begin at the edge that overextends, on the side, and follow the trace mark.

The strip should just spiral out.

ATTACHING BIAS BINDING ON ONE SIDE

This technique is used to finish the hems on a garment. It is useful because the bias binding is completely concealed on the wrong side of the garment.

STEP 1

With right sides together, lay the edge of the bias binding over the edge of the fabric being finished.

Stitch evenly ¼ inch in from the edge (see the accompanying diagram).

STEP 2

Turn the bias binding the wrong side of the fabric so that the edge of the binding is slightly set back (see the accompanying diagram).

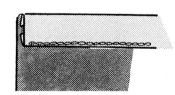

Sew the other edge of the bias binding in place using a slip stitch.

ATTACHING BIAS BINDING OVER AN EDGE

In this version, the bias binding will be visible on both the wrong and the right sides of the fabric.

This method is used to edge rounded pieces on clothing or decorative articles.

STEP 1

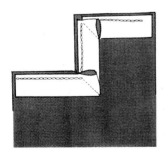

Line up the bias binding and the fabric edge to edge. Place the right side of the bias binding tape, unfolded, against the right side of the fabric. Stitch into the crease of the first outer fold of the bias binding, or ¾ inch from the edge.

STEP 2

Turn under the bias binding onto the wrong side of the fabric.

Fix it in place using a machine stitch, or better yet, set it in by hand using a small hemstitch.

ATTACHING BIAS BINDING AT CORNERS

Corners that are to be edged by bias binding should be perfectly finished. If this is not the case, the whole piece will suffer. As with all finishing, the application of bias binding requires precision.

STEP 1

First, pin the bias binding onto the edge of the item so that the right side of the binding is against the right side of the fabric as in Step 1 of the previous procedure.

STEP 2

Bend or fold back excess bias binding along the corners to create triangular pockets (see the accompanying diagram).

STEP 3

When you start stitching, fold down these triangular pockets down and orient them toward the bottom. Clip the corners using a pair of narrow scissors.

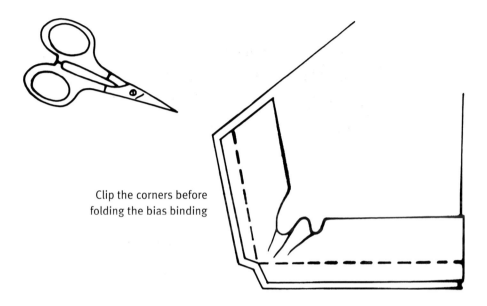

Clip the corners before folding the bias binding

STEP 4

Turn under the bias binding toward the wrong side of the fabric while making sure that the corners are square. Stitch by machine or sew by hand using a hem stitch.

ON THE SEWING MACHINE

It is important that you work with the right machine foot for attaching bias binding, i.e., that it is not only appropriate for the technique but also for the type of binding you have chosen.

For bias binding that has not been prefolded, including binding that you have cut and made yourself, use a binder foot. This accessory will allow you to obtain better quality results.

On the other hand, if you are working with prefolded or ready-to-attach bias binding that you purchased in the shop, the standard presser foot for straight seams should be quite sufficient.

Table Place Mats

The two table place mat models presented here are easy to make. The invigorating colors of their bias-bound edges make them perfect for the kitchen table or the garden table. Ticking, which is used for this project, is particularly hardwearing and very affordable. The methods described below can also be applied to tablecloths, centerpiece doilies, and other kinds of table toppers.

YOU WILL NEED

(for two place mats)
100% cotton ticking, 14 inches by 36 inches
Prefolded cotton bias binding, 4 yards of ⅞-inch-wide fabric and in a lively, contrasting color
Sewing thread, in a color that matches the bias binding
Fine pins
Plastic triangle
Yardstick
Tailor's chalk
Dressmaker's scissors

HELPFUL HINTS

Even if the guidelines for assembling these models sound simple to you, you still might need to set aside extra time to make them depending upon your fabric choice and the quality of the finishing that you desire. Take your time as you work.

FABRIC DIMENSIONS

Each of the place mats measures 18 inches by 14 inches. This is a standard size, but you can modify it according to your own tastes and the dimensions of your table.

To obtain the required length of fabric, multiply the width of a place mat by the number of place mats that you want and add on a bit of excess to be on the safe side.

CUTTING THE FABRIC

The Place Mat with Rounded Corners

On the wrong side of the fabric, trace a rectangle measuring 18 inches by 14 inches. Cut along the trace marks. Fold the fabric rectangle in four so that the four corners overlap.

Round out all of them at the same time using a pair of scissors so that the curves will be identical to each other.

The Place Mat with Notched Corners

On the wrong side of the fabric, trace a rectangle measuring 18 inches by 14 inches. Cut out the rectangle along the trace marks.

Trace a small square measuring 2 inches by 2 inches on each of the four corners. Remove these small fabric squares; the bias binding will be applied along the notches you created.

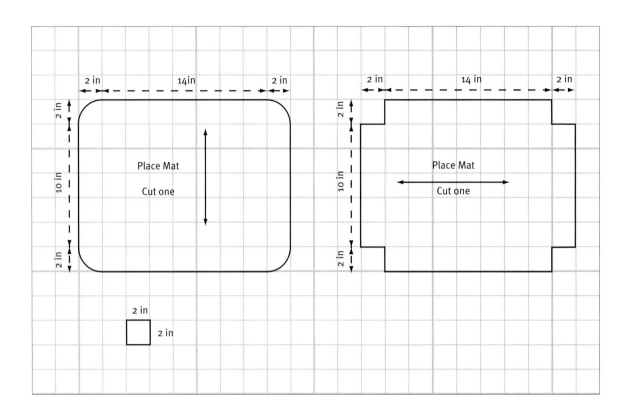

2 in   14 in   2 in   2 in   14 in   2 in

2 in   10 in   2 in

Place Mat

Cut one

2 in

2 in

THE PLACE MAT WITH ROUNDED CORNERS IN 2 STEPS

Most of the effort here involves working the four corners in a symmetric way so that neither the fabric nor the bias binding ends up puckering when you are done.

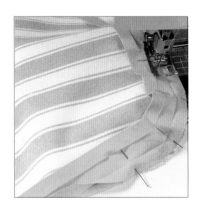

1

ATTACHING THE FIRST EDGE OF THE BIAS BINDING

Matching outer edges, lay the opened-out bias binding on the wrong side of the place mat fabric, with the right side of bias tape facing down. Pin all around the place mat, then carefully stitch along the crease of the outer fold (see "Attaching Bias Binding over an Edge" and the diagram on page 224).

ATTACHING THE SECOND EDGE OF THE BIAS BINDING

Fold over the bias binding onto the right side of the fabric.

Pin it in and sew it in place using as even a stitch as you can make. Work in "slow mode." Because of its flexibility, the bias binding should take on the rounded profile of the corners. Make sure that the corners are in perfect symmetry.

THE PLACE MAT WITH NOTCHED CORNERS IN 2 STEPS

The triangular pockets that are created in the bias binding (see page 224) should make it possible for you to edge the right angles of the corner notches.

ATTACHING THE FIRST EDGE OF THE BIAS BINDING

Pin the first side of the strip of the bias binding, right sides together, to the edge of the place mat. For the corners, guide the extra bias binding underneath the machine foot so that you create small triangular pockets.

Stitch while turning the excess bias binding downward. Clip the corners (see "Attaching Bias Binding at Corners" on page 224).

SEWING THE BACK OF THE PLACE MAT

Fold the strip of bias binding to the wrong side of the place mat, making sure that the four notched corners are square and even.

Sew all around the edge of the place mat by hand, using a hemstitch. Flatten the triangular pockets using an iron and carefully fold the bias binding around the corners.

Attaching Piping

PRELIMINARIES

Piping is a decorative strip of material consisting of a flat and a rounded part. In the notions shop you can find various kinds of ready-to-apply piping. If you do not find a strip or a braid that is appropriate for your item, here is how to proceed in order to create your own piping using a fabric of your choice and a piece of piping cord.

MORE ABOUT THE TECHNIQUE

Making piping is somewhat like making bias binding because you cut the bias strips for it from the same fabric that you used to complete the main piece or from a coordinating fabric. However, with piping, the bias-cut fabric is wrapped around a cord. The way you apply it is different as well. For more see the steps that follow.

STEP 1

Begin by cutting an unbroken strip, on the bias, from the fabric that you have selected (see how to cut a bias strip on page 222).

STEP 2

Buy piping cord (or cable cord) of a diameter suited to your article, and place it in the center of the bias strip you have cut.

With wrong sides together, fold the bias strip around the cord, matching the long cut edges.

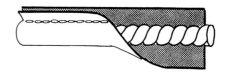

STEP 3

Pin the long edges of the bias strip together. The extended flat part of the piping should be at least   inch in width beyond the rounded part.

STEP 4

Place the piping foot (or zipper foot) on the sewing machine. Stitch along the cord, close to it, but without catching the stitches in it.

STEP 5

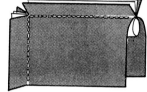

Now you are ready to attach the piping to your item.

Pin the flat part of the piping toward the top of the right side of one of the fabric pieces.

Guide the piping around the corners using the piping (zipper) foot of the sewing machine.

STEP 6

With the piping seam along the desired seamline, stitch to fasten the piping onto this first piece of fabric.

STEP 7

Continue by setting the next fabric piece in place, right sides together with the piping sandwiched between. Stitch on the flat of the piping, as close to the corded part as possible.

STEP 8

Notch the corners and turn the item over onto its right side. The piping should edge the contour of the pieces that you have assembled so far.

ON THE SEWING MACHINE

A few sewing machine manufacturers offer, besides the zipper foot, a special piping foot. You should give preference to the latter since it allows you to work with two needles simultaneously: The first needle stitches along the cord, and the second stitches along the flat of the piping.

If you do not own this accessory, use the zipper foot to first make one seam, then the other.

The Curtain Tieback

Piping can be used to throw the contours of a seam into relief. In this project, it is used to accentuate the round profile of a curtain tieback. It is certainly possible to imagine finishing that gives definition to articles with features that tend to wear out, like the contour of a bag, the edges of a sofa cushion, or the cuff of a coat.

YOU WILL NEED

Heavyweight (upholstery) cotton, for one tieback, 10 inches by 27½ inches
Cotton pique, for lining, 10 inches by 27½ inches, plus extra for piping (see "Choosing a Fabric")
Piping cording, 3½ yards in length by ¼ inch in diameter
Drapery thread
Fine pins
Yardstick
Tailor's chalk
Dressmaker's scissors

HELPFUL HINTS

Piping can be used to finish an article in ways that range from the classic to the modern. By playing on shape and color, you can achieve some surprising results. Let the laws of harmony guide you in the choices you make.

FABRIC DIMENSIONS

The finished tieback measures 25½ inches in length by 8 inches in height. Change these measurements if you need to. A tieback is often lined in a more lightweight fabric for added durability. However, there is no rule against using the main fabric for lining material either.

CUTTING THE FABRIC

Fold the fabric in half with right sides together. Set the center of the pattern piece over the fabric fold. Pin it, then trace out the contours of the curtain tieback.

Do the same thing on the wrong side of the lining fabric. Then cut out the two pieces adding a ⅝-inch seam allowance around the trace marks.

CHOOSING A FABRIC

The fabric used for the front of the tieback is a very thick fabric. For this curtain tieback it is preferable to cut the bias strip covering the piping cord from the same fabric as the lining (cotton pique) so you can make your own matching button loop. If you do opt for purchased piping, purchase a narrow upholstery cord to match, to use for the button loops, or make your own button loops.

If you do make your own piping, make sure to purchase an additional 24 inches worth of lining fabric so that you can use it to cover the piping cord.

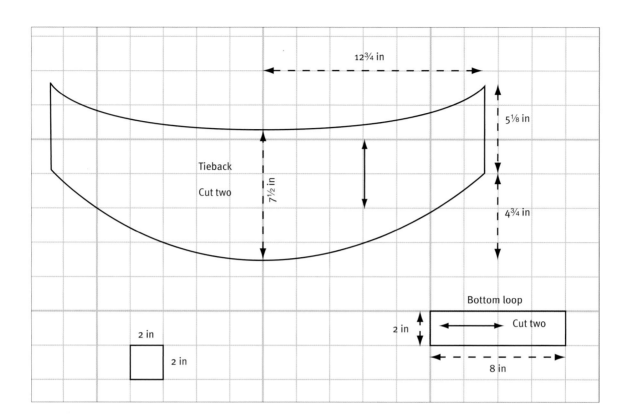

12¾ in

5⅛ in

Tieback

Cut two

7½ in

4¾ in

Bottom loop

2 in

Cut two

2 in

2 in

2 in

8 in

THE CURTAIN TIEBACK
IN 4 STEPS

This step-by-step guide can be followed to create a single curtain tieback. For a pair of tiebacks, you only have to repeat these steps once again. If the fabric has a pattern, do not forget to reorient the material for symmetry the second time around.

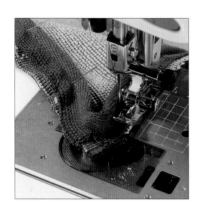

1

ATTACHING THE PIPING

Place the zipper (cording) foot on your sewing machine. Lay the piping over the right side of the front tieback piece with the flat seam allowance extending outward. Baste, then stitch.

At the corners, leave the needle in the fabric, lifting the presser foot to pivot and clipping the seam allowance to turn the corner, then continue working. The bias strip of piping should naturally follow the curves of the tieback.

2 HOW TO FINISH ATTACHING THE PIPING

To finish attaching the piping, position the terminal end over the beginning end while pointing the piping away from the tieback. Once they have been set in place, the ends of the piping are sewn into the seams used for adding the lining.

Complete a second seam ⅛ inch from the edges to attach the flat part of the piping to the tieback.

3 ATTACHING THE LINING

With the right sides of the fabrics together, lay the lining on top of the piped tieback, with the piping sandwiched between. Pin the lining in place. Stitch all along the edge of the piping, leaving a 6-inch opening along one side for turning. Trim the corners, clip the seam allowances at the top rounded edge, and notch the lower rounded edge of the tieback and lining.

Turn the tieback right side out. Turn under the raw edges at the opening and press. Close the opening with a slip stitch.

4 SEWING THE BUTTON LOOPS

Make two pieces of corded tube (see "A Dressmaker's Trick," page 231). Slip the ends of the loop fasteners into the gap between the wrong sides of the cotton front tieback and the lining on each side of the tieback.

If necessary, undo a few stitches of the seam. Using small backstitches, firmly attach the loop fasteners by hand to finish the piece.

FINISHING

The button loops that you make for the tieback to match the piping will leave an impression of continuity that can successfully unify all the elements of this item.

You might also consider making the button loops out of satin ribbon or any other braid that is available in a matching color.

235

The Drawstring Closure

PRELIMINARIES

A drawstring closure consists of a wide casing or top hem into which a cord or an elastic is inserted for tightening or tying off part of an item; this cord may remain invisible or extend out of the casing, in which case the closure would be secured with a knot. Not only can you find this kind of work on garments—for example, the waistlines of pants, skirts, or dresses—but also as a decorative feature on all sorts of pouches or cases, usually closed off by a knotted ribbon.

MORE ABOUT THE TECHNIQUE

Making a drawstring waistband in and of itself is not difficult to do. However, if you decide to add one to your item, you must make allowances for it from the very beginning when you purchase the fabric and cut out the pattern pieces. The height of the casing, especially, should suit the type of item you are working on, be it a garment or a pouch.

Therefore, take careful measurements.

STEP 1

At the top of your work, fold ¾ inch to the wrong side of the fabric using an iron. Press a second fold of the same height (this may vary depending upon the type of article) over the previous fold. Pin it in place.

STEP 2

Stitch along the bottom of this casing, inch from the folded edge. Leave the two ends of the casing open.

STEP 3

Using a safety pin of a size that fits through the waistband, thread the elastic, or a drawstring about ⅜ inch in diameter, through the waistband casing, making sure that the elastic lies flat.

When it comes time to sew the waistband, check that the elastic lies flat all around the circumference of the garment before you start to stitch the casing. The elastic may have the tendency of curling back on itself, meaning that it will be hard to fix a mistake once the casing has been sewn shut.

A DRESSMAKER'S TRICK

The height of the casing should be at least ¼ inch greater than the width of the elastic (or the drawstring) that it will enclose. If you do not make this allowance, it will be difficult for you to slide in a new cord when you need to replace one that has worn out or broken. This ease also makes it possible for you to smooth out parts of the elastic that become gathered anywhere around the case, even after it has been sewn shut.

STEP 4

If you are using elastic, overlap the ends by 1 inches. Stitch them together securely. Move the elastic through the casing so the joining falls at the back or the side of the casing to avoid a bulge at the front. Even out any gathers along the length of the elastic and sew the opening closed.

If you are using a cord, leave 6-inch ends hanging loose for ties. Tie a knot on each end to prevent the cord ends from becoming lost inside the casing.

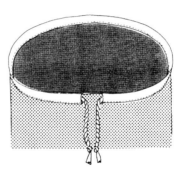

ON THE SEWING MACHINE

If you are using a flat elastic, even out all the gathers to the best of your ability so that it will be less likely to bunch up with prolonged use. Insert a pin in the center front and the center back of each side. The pins should run through both the fabric and the cord.

Use a single straight stitch to keep them together. Set the stitch length to ⅛ inch and proceed rapidly, starting from the center of the casing. Stretch the cord out taut and firmly hold onto the sections of the cord that come just before and after the presser foot.

Once you have finished stitching, remove the pins.

The Summer Pants

Here is an item that you will be happy to have during the dog days of summer! This pair of pants is lightweight and makes for a quick, easy project that you can finish in an hour or less – that includes cutting the fabric and assembly. Also, it fits both children and adults; all you have to do is adjust the pattern to an appropriate size. Even the crotch area, which usually requires the most delicate, careful work when making a pair of pants, requires very little effort for this project.

YOU WILL NEED

Blue-striped cotton fabric, 2½ yards by 44–45 inches wide
Flat elastic, 1⅛ yards by 0.98 inch wide, in white
Sewing thread, in a color that matches the pants fabric
Safety pin, for inserting the cord into the casing
Fine pins
Plastic triangle
Yardstick
Tailor's chalk
Dressmaker's scissors

MEASUREMENTS
Take the waist and hip measurements of the model (see helpful hints on page 247).

Take the center front and the center back measurements from the waist down to the ground, as well as the length from the waist down to the ground at the side of the leg.

Adjust the sizes of the pattern pieces according to these measurements.

FABRIC DIMENSIONS
To make pants from a fabric that is without nap and which measures either 44–45 inches or 55 inches in width, you should allow for a length that is equal to two times the finished length of the pants plus 6 inches for the casing and the hems.

Because of the way it is cut and because of the drawstring closure, this pair of pants does not have seams along its sides and is thus very easy to make. However, for the pants to fit you well, they must drape smoothly and be loose-fitting. This is why it is necessary to add 6 inches to the hip measurement of the two pieces to make a garment that is comfortable to wear.

HELPFUL HINTS

This pattern can be used as a point of departure for other types of pants. Cut it to the knee and it can become a pair of Bermuda shorts. Cut it further up for very comfortable short pants or at midcalf for pedal pushers. You can also make it reversible or add pockets, but simply using an unusual fabric is enough to make it appealing.

CUTTING THE FABRIC

The originality of this pattern and its simplicity derive especially from the fact that each leg is tailored from one and the same piece of fabric.

To cut, fold the fabric in half, right sides together, and pin the whole pattern onto the wrong side (do not place the pattern fold line over the fabric fold). Trace along the outlines and mark the assembling points.

The seam allowances, including the allowances for the drawstring closure (see the dotted-line in the diagram below), are already included in the pattern measurements.

size 40 pants

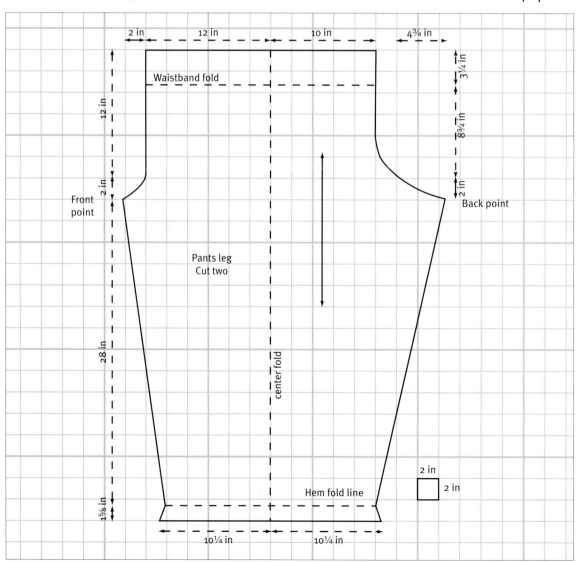

THE SUMMER PANTS
IN 4 STEPS

Check one last time to make sure that you have an appropriate pants length. Then carefully overcast the edge of the two pieces before proceeding to the steps that follow.

1 JOINING THE LEGS

Since each leg is made from a single piece of cloth, fold each of the leg pieces in half lengthwise with the right sides of the fabric together.

Make sure that the two leg edges and the assembly markings coincide precisely with each other. Pin, then stitch ⅝ inch from the edge. Press the seams open with an iron.

2 COMPLETING THE CROTCH

Turn one of the two legs inside out so the right side faces outward. Slide one leg into the other with right sides together; make sure that the interior seams coincide.

Pin back the edges together from the point to the top, then stitch (see how to sew a rounded seam on page 65). Repeat on front edges; stitch to the top of the elastic, or for cord casing, see page 242. Then trim seam allowances ¼ inch from the seam. Press the seam open with an iron.

3 MAKING THE CASING

With the pair of pants wrong side out, use an iron to turn in a 1⅜-inch hem fold along the waistline. Create another fold of the same size over the first. Pin, then stitch along the bottom edge ⅛ inch above the edge of the fold.

Leave a 2-inch opening along the front side of the pants to insert the elastic.

INSERTING THE ELASTIC

Pin the safety pin through one end of the elastic. Slide it through the casing using the technique usually used with gathers.

Let the elastic ends overlap each other by 1⅛ inches and stitch them together firmly. Push the elastic back into the casing and sew the casing shut.

FINISHING

Before you work on the bottom hemline of the summer pants, turn the pair over onto its right side and try it on.

On the bottom of each leg, create an initial ⅝-inch fold inward. Then fold once again to create a defined hem.

Make sure the general-purpose foot has been installed into the sewing machine, then pin and stitch.

For cord casing, work Step 2, stitching the front seam up to 2¾ inches from the top. Press the seam allowance under on each side of this top opening, and topstitch along each side of the opening ⅛ inch from the edge. Complete the casing as in Step 3, but omit the elastic opening when you stitch the lower edge of the casing in place. Thread the cord through the casing, leaving the ends hanging at front; tie a knot at each end of the cord.

THE CARE AND MAINTENANCE OF YOUR FABRICS

Fabric Care

WASHING

Fabrics may or may not withstand certain treatments, depending upon the composition of their fibers. Unfortunately, labels on garment fabrics sold by the yard do not always provide all the necessary information. On the other hand, the selvages of a good number of fabrics intended for decorative articles include maintenance instructions. Also, nowadays such information tends to be standardized.

In case the fabric that you used for your garment did not come with maintenance instructions when you purchased it, here are the main principles you should pay attention to.

Linens, which consist of somewhat loose, woven fibers and which are often used for constructing garments, should be washed at a maximum temperature of 140 degrees Fahrenheit (140°F). Varieties that are meant for bed or table linen and which have a "100% linen" indication may be washed at temperatures up to 194°F and should support mild chlorine bleaching if they are colorfast.

White cottons can be machine-washed at temperatures between 86°F and 194°F. Please note that today's detergents work more effectively at a lower temperature, between 32°F and 140°F. White cottons can be treated with chlorine bleach if they become stained.

Colored cottons can be washed in the same manner as white cottons so long as they are colorfast. If you are not sure about whether the colors will run, wash the colored cottons separately.

Knit or woven wools can be machine-washed with cold water if the washing machine has a delicate cycle. Use detergent that is suitable for delicate washing. If you are washing a wool item by hand, use soap flakes with cold water. Rinse thoroughly.

Do not wring the item; instead, pat it dry in a terry towel. Then spread it out as flat as you can for drying.

Silks should be washed using appropriate, specific techniques; they should only be washed by hand with cold or tepid water and soap flakes. Never scrub silks; instead, press on them. Do not wring a silk item; instead, dry it by gently rolling it in a terry towel. If you have any doubts, have your dry cleaner clean your silk item for you.

Viscose rayon can be machine-washed; you should set the machine to cold wash and the setting to delicate items.

Acrylic fabrics should be treated in the same manner as viscose rayon, but note that they sometimes tend to pill. Run an electric razor over the surface of these fabrics to remove the lint or pills.

Polyamides come in a variety of textures. You can find fabric varieties that are woven as well as knit. They can be machine-washed at a temperature of 86°F. The primary drawback of these fabrics is that they tend to yellow, the effect of which is especially noticed on fabrics that come in light colors. Never dry items made from these fabrics in the sun.

Polyesters can be machine-washed at a low temperature (104°F at the greatest). Be careful when drying them; if you are too vigorous, you can leave permanent marks on the surface of these fabrics.

Microfiber fabrics can be machine-washed at a temperature of 86°F. They dry very quickly and do not require any pressing.

Velvet can consist of a variety of fibers: cotton, linen, wool, silk, or synthetic silk. They should be washed very gently to ensure that the pile does not get crushed.

Always turn the wrong side of velvet items out (pile facing in) before placing them into the drum of the washing machine. How you wash these items depends upon the composition of the fibers, but, to keep colors from running, do not wash them at a temperature above 104°F.

STAIN REMOVAL

Some stains resist washing. Treat the stain as early as you can. When a stain occurs, first try to blot as much of it as you can with a rag or a paper towel. Do not rub the paper towel against the surface of the fabric, or you risk leaving pill behind. Rinse the item in cold water, and let it dry. Finally, if necessary, apply a chemical stain remover.

Simple, Useful Stain Removal Methods

TYPE OF STAIN	WHAT TO APPLY	DIRECTIONS
Candle wax	Detergent	Harden the stain with ice cubes, scrape, then wash
Coffee, chocolate, tea, red wine, fruit juice, soda	Fresh stains: rinse with water Older stains: detergent	Let the item soak in clean water, then rinse
Sauces, jam, ice cream	Detergent	Rinse the item in water while rubbing; let it soak for a few hours before washing
Fat or grease	Detergent	Dampen the item and let it stand for a few hours; wash, then scrub it on the wrong and right sides
Milk and dairy products	Water + 1 tablespoon of 8% (3 dl/0.63 pt) ammonia	Scrub the item, then soak and wash it
Blood	Fresh stains: cold water Older stains: cold water + 2 tablespoons of coarse salt per quart	Rinse the item, let it stay moist for a few hours, then scrub and wash it

Pressing

PRESSING EQUIPMENT

Good pressing requires knowledge of a few key principles but a minimum of equipment. Here are the essential tools:

A **steam iron** with a steam release button and a pressing button which will cause the release of pressurized steam. The iron should not be too lightweight. If the iron is not heavy enough, you will have to apply a greater amount of downward pressure when pressing out creases.

A wide **ironing board** that is constructed with a grill so that the steam can pass right through without dampening the board covering. The covering should be made of thick cotton. Lay a few more layers of covering over the board covering if you need them. Avoid boards that have asbestos coatings; at present their use is generally prohibited by law. The board should include a place, usually at one of the ends, for you to set down the iron.

A **sleeve board** for ironing narrow or rounded items. It usually consists of a small board with a free leg and also has a covering.

A **pressing cloth** made of white, non-pilling cotton that you should wash beforehand to remove any finishes.

A **water spray bottle** so that you can spray cotton or linen fabrics which are easier to iron when damp.

Ironing spray containing some kind of finish to ease the task of ironing certain fibers (see below).

A FEW IRONING TIPS

Linen should be pressed with an extremely hot iron while it is damp. While pressing, use a pressing cloth to work on recalcitrant creases and an ironing spray for table cloths and napkins.

White cotton should be pressed while it is still damp. If the item is dry, give it a few sprays from the water spray bottle. Use an ironing spray when pressing table linen (see above).

Colored cotton should be pressed while it is still damp. If it is not colorfast, place a piece of white cotton between the coating of the ironing board and the surface of the fabric. This will help you avoid leaving a stain on the ironing board. Before you wash, test the color quality of the fabric. Press the wrong side of a hem with a pressing cloth that is slightly damp. If the fabric leaves marks on the cloth, this means that the item is not colorfast.

Woven wool should be pressed with the iron set to a medium temperature. Place a dry pressing cloth between the sole of the iron and the wool surface of your item to prevent a sheen or lustering.

Knit wool should not be pressed since that risks flattening or stretching the fabric. Suspend the knit item from a hanger, set the iron to its "cotton" setting, then release a jet of steam onto the surface of the item. Never put the sole of the iron in contact with the wool surface.

You should press **silk** only when it is very damp; press it on the wrong side with an iron set to a medium temperature. Avoid using steam on the right side of the item to prevent sheen or lustering on the surface of the fabric. Avoid using an ironing spray, which may stain the silk.

Viscose rayon should be pressed with a tepid iron; press the wrong side of the item with a pressing cloth that is slightly damp.

Synthetic silks should be pressed on their wrong side with a tepid iron. Some polyesters do not require any pressing.

Velvet should be pressed on the wrong side and laid on top of a thick covering such as a bath towel to keep the pile from being crushed. After pressing, turn the garment onto its right side and shake it.

CLEANING THE IRON

You must service your iron regularly. The most important step you can take is to clean the sole, since heat might have resulted in the accumulation of lint, pile, and bonding agents from fusible products.

To do this, set the iron to the "silk" setting and rub the sole with a damp rag that has been soaked in spirit alcohol. You should also find specific products for cleaning the sole at the store. You should definitely stay away from abrasive substances, however.

Try to use demineralized water to fill steam irons. Tap water is not in and of itself bad, but you will have to descale the iron regularly. To descale the interior of the iron, put the iron into the "cotton" setting. Dilute a dose of spirit vinegar with water in a one-to-two ratio. Pour this mixture into the iron. Disconnect the iron and lay it down flat onto a soup plate; let the mixture drain out of the iron, removing any tartar accumulation with it.

Repeat the process to remove all the accumulated tartar completely. Special products are available just for descaling steam irons.

Taking Measurements for Garments

A Few General Guidelines

The measurements that you take determine the size of the pattern and, consequently, the amount of fabric to use. Verify your measurements from time to time as you work, and correct them as necessary. When you start compare them against the indications printed on the pattern envelope. Note that, depending upon where the patterns come from (Europe, the United States, etc.), there may be slight variations in shoulder widths and body heights.

If you need to take the measurements for yourself, do not hesitate to get help. Proceed as follows:
— Dress only in your undergarments, but keep your shoes on
— Tie a thin ribbon around your waist. The ribbon should be neither too loose nor too tight. Keep this ribbon for reference around your waist as you make all your other measurements;
— Use your tape measure smoothly
— Stand up as straight as you can, let your arms hang along the sides of your body and set your feet slightly apart, with balanced hips.

HEIGHTWISE MEASUREMENTS

The **back waist length** is the length of the span between the base of the neck and the ribbon around your waist; the front chest length is between the base of the neck and the waistline ribbon.

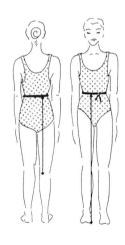

To make skirts, take your skirt length, which extends from your waistline down to the crook of your knees. For pants, consider a pants length extending from your waistline down to the ground.

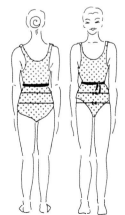

CIRCUMFERENTIAL MEASUREMENTS

You can take your **bust measurement** by setting the start of your tape measure against the tip of a breast, wrapping it around your bust, running it underneath your armpits and bringing it back around to join the start of the tape. Your **waist measurement** corresponds to the length of the ribbon that was wrapped around your waist.

You can take your **hip measurement** in two steps. Begin by taking the measurement for the high hip, which corresponds to the circumference of the pelvis at the point where the hips jut out. To take the measurement for the full hips, go around the fullest point of the buttocks.

While you take these measurements, make sure that you keep the measuring tape horizontal.

LENGTHWISE MEASUREMENTS

These measurements are essential for garments like a long-sleeved dress, a blouse, a vest, or a coat.

The **length of the arms** is measured with your arms bent, at a right angle and in two steps. First you measure from your shoulder to your elbow, then from your elbow to your wrist.

Taking Measurements for Decorative Articles

A Few General Guidelines

In decorative sewing, taking measurements is also a very important step. Good measurements will make it possible for you to fit your patterns to your furniture and various aspects of your decor with precision. Some of them can be read right off the articles that you already own if you are just attempting to replace one of them.

However, if you are working on an entirely new addition, here is how you should proceed with your measurements.

BED LINEN

Whether you are working on flat sheets, comforter slipcovers, bedspreads, or pillowcases, simple techniques for calculating relevant measurements are already available to you.

For **flat sheets,** you should consult your mattress label for length, width, and height indications.

The length of the sheet = the length of the mattress + twice the mattress thickness + 20 inches for the edging + 5 inches for the hems, of which $3\frac{1}{4}$ to 4 inches is for the fold. The width of the sheet = the width of the mattress + twice the mattress thickness + 20 inches for the edging + $1\frac{1}{2}$ inches for the hems on the side.

For a **comforter slipcover,** take down the length and the width of the comforter.

The length of the case = the length of the comforter + $\frac{3}{8}$ inch as a seam allowance + $1\frac{3}{8}$ inches as a hem allowance.

The width of the case = the width of the comforter + $\frac{3}{8}$ inch as a seam allowance.

If the case requires a faced edging, add 4 inches to the length.

To take measurements for a **bedspread,** first dress it with all the sheets, the comforter, blankets and any pillows you would need.

The length of the bedspread = the length of the dressed bed + 10 inches of excess in all, on each end + $\frac{3}{8}$ inch as a seam allowance. The width of the bed-spread = the width of the dressed bed + 20 inches of drop in all (a drop of 9.84 inches on each side) + $\frac{3}{8}$ inch as a seam allowance.

Take note of the following for **pillowcases:**

The length of the pillowcase should equal twice the length of the pillow + 8 inches.

The width of the pillowcase should equal twice the width of the pillow + $\frac{3}{8}$ inch as a seam allowance.

If you want a pillowcase with a flat frill that measures $2\frac{3}{8}$ inches wide, add an extra $4\frac{3}{4}$ inches to both the length and the width.

For a **cushion case** (bed, chair, armchair, or sofa), refer to the indications that come with the item.

Cushions can come in different shapes. Square or rectangular varieties are often assembled the same way that a buttoned pillowcase is, only the latter is decorated.

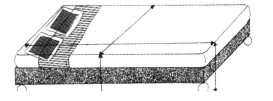

To make measurements for a cushion, see the instructions for the pillowcase on page 248.

WINDOW DRESSING

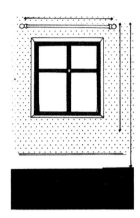

In order to take exact measurements, the curtain rod should first be installed. The necessary length of fabric will be determined by measuring from the rod.

For **curtains that are going to be lined,** you should use the same dimensions on the lining material as you do for the main fabric.

The height of the curtain = the span between the bottom of the curtain rod and the hem of the curtain (wherever you want) + the height of the heading (depending upon the model you have chosen) + the height of the hem (in general, 2 inches) for lightweight curtains and between 3 inches and 4 inches for a double curtain).

To make **long curtains** that reach the ground, subtract ⅝ inch from the primary height so that the curtain itself does not brush the floor, then add on the heights of the heading and the hem.
The width of the curtains = three times the length of the curtain rod + 2 inches for the side hems.
The width of the lined curtains = twice the length of the curtain rod + 4 inches for the side hems.

To take measurements for a **curtain tieback,** wrap the measuring tape around the drawn curtain so that it functions the same way the finished tieback would, and extend it back to the wall where the hooks will be.

The length of the tieback = the measurement of the drawn curtain + ⅜ inch as a seam allowance. The width of the tieback depends upon the weight of the fabric; on average it should be 2 times some width between 3¼ inches and 5¼ inches + ⅜ inch as a seam allowance.

For **roller window shades,** measurements should be taken on site at the window as you would do with curtains. Your measurements also depend upon the rolling mechanism used with the shade. Generally, the height of the shade = the length of the span from the top of the window down to the sill + 1¼ inches for attaching the fabric to the rolling mechanism + 2½ inches for the bottom hem.

The width of the shade = the width of the window at the sill + 2 inches for the hems at the side.

TABLE LINEN

Tablecloths. From the simple tablecloth that drapes down to half the table height to the formal tablecloth that drapes down to the floor, tablecloths may be as long as you want and come in any shape or size. Two of the most common sets of measurements are given on page 58.

Table napkins are usually square, but you should also be able to find rectangular models. However, they may vary in size depending upon how they are used; thus tea napkins are usually smaller than dinner napkins (see page 58).

A Glossary of Commonly Used Fabrics

As with any other kind of hands-on pursuit, sewing has its own language. Below is a list of the principal terms of this language. Even if they do not all sound as enchanting as taffeta, chintz, or organza, each has a specific meaning that you should become acquainted with. Be sure to also refer to the section on fabric compositions on page 11.

Chintz is a cotton fabric that has been treated with a finish. The finish is meant to glaze the surface of the fabric and keep dust from getting caught between the fibers. Chintz is used decoratively for making seat coverings.

Damask is a fabric that usually comes in one or two colors whose decorative appeal lies in the interplay of warp and weft.

Denim is a thick cotton twill weave that is traditionally dyed in an indigo-based dye. It came into fashion years ago and has appealed to generations ever since.

Gabardine is made from either wool or cotton. The right side of the weave is characterized by a distinct slanted ribbing. It is a sturdy fabric with a twill weave which is used in many articles, including among others, raincoats and sports apparel.

Ikat or chiné is a dyeing or printing technique based on tying either the warp or the weft threads (or both), so that the tied-up parts of the threads do not absorb the dye.

Interlock is a run-resistant hosiery-type fabric that is knit into two layers and which features two jersey faces.

Jersey is a knitted fabric which has a topside consisting of plain (knit) stitches and an underside consisting of purl stitches.

Muslin, once used to describe fine silk fabrics, now is commonly used to mean cotton fabric often used for making pillow forms, to fit inside pillow covers.

Organdy is a fine, transparent cotton fabric whose surface is heavily starched to give it stiffness. Organdy absolutely must be re-starched after each washing.

Organza is a transparent, heavily starched fabric made from fine silk.

The **plain weave** is the name given to a simple construction technique involving the interweaving of the warp and weft threads, regardless of what kind of thread is used: The straight grain (or lengthwise grain) runs perpendicular to the crosswise grain.

Pongee is a plain weave fabric made from silk. Pongee is typically used for lining garments.

Satin is a fabric that has a lustrous face and a slubbed face. This effect is produced by the weave (see this term) that is used.

Serge is a type of weave characterized by parallel diagonal ridges. The most well known serge is denim.

Silk dupion is a fabric known for its granular surface. This name is also given to synthetic silks that have textured surfaces.

Taffeta is a fabric made from silk or synthetic fibers and has a lustrous surface and a crisp feel.

Tweed is a plain or serge woven fabric that is made from irregular-looking yarns.

Velvet has a tight, short pile surface on one side and a plain weave surface on the reverse. Depending upon the types of fiber that it is woven from, velvet may be used in apparel as well as in home furnishing.

The **weave** of a fabric refers to the way the weft and warp yarns are interlaced. The plain weave is the simplest weave.

A Glossary of Sewing Threads

Sewing threads come in spools of varying sizes that range from the cone to the tube. Each variety of thread serves its own specific purposes. The first rule you should keep in mind is to use a thread that is the same as that of the fabric so that all the elements of the resulting piece will react identically to washing and wear and tear. Therefore use a 100% cotton thread on cotton fabrics, polyester thread on synthetic fabrics, etc.

The following rules concern the thickness and the length of thread. Information regarding the composition, length, and thickness of the thread should be inscribed on the adjoining label. The figure that indicates the thickness corresponds to the number of kilometers in one kilogram of the given thread. For example, the number 50 would mean that a kilogram of this thread would contain 50 kilometers of it. The higher the number, the finer the thread.

Basting thread comes in large bobbins. The thread is delicate and is used for preparing seams and putting together various pieces; its stitches are easily undone.

Silk or **cotton buttonhole twist** comes in a small tube-shaped spool. Its "twisted" appearance means that it is perfect for embroidering buttonholes by hand, for attaching buttons, or for topstitching decorative details onto thick woolen fabrics.

Heirloom thread is made from two strands. It comes on a tube-shaped spool and is principally used for assembling lightweight fabrics.

Machine buttonhole thread is made of 100% polyester and can be used to make buttonholes on the sewing machine. It is a cheaper version of the buttonhole twist.

100% cotton **machine embroidery thread** is ideal for working on topstitches, buttonholes, or novelty embroidering. Several thicknesses of the thread are available (sizes 30, 50, and 60) for you to use, depending upon the thickness of the fabric.

Polyester or "all purpose" thread is recommended for assembling synthetic fabrics, mixed fabrics, and knit fabrics. The texture of this thread appears irregular. It is used solely in machine sewing because when used in hand sewing it has the tendency to twist and create knots. The polyester which is used to make this thread responds poorly to high temperature pressing as well as washing at temperatures higher than 140°F.

Twisted or mercerized thread is 100% cotton and perfect for machine seams. Always keep size 50 (the standard thickness) thread handy in your sewing box for the purpose of assembling cotton fabrics.

Stranded cotton or cotton floss is a durable six-stranded 100% cotton thread with a dull appearance. It is available in sizes 20 to 120, depending upon the support thickness that is required. This thread is used with hand sewing as well as machine sewing. It is also called "special drapery thread" and is used in assembling woolen fabrics.

Viscose thread has the same qualities as the preceding thread but it is used with synthetic fabrics. It can be used to create lustrous looking embroidery work.

Wool yarn comes in flat spools. Its strong durability allows you to produce sturdy hand-sewn seams and to securely attach metal shank buttons.

A Glossary of Sewing Terms

ASSEMBLY refers to the joining of several pieces of fabric using a straight stitch.

An **ALLOWANCE** is the excess fabric that is left between a seam and the edge of the fabric; it may be used for later modifications, for the completion of an additional seam, or simply as a means of preserving the structure of the assembly.

BASTING means using a basting stitch to assemble several pieces temporarily to give you a chance to test out the fit of the item and decide upon subsequent corrective measures. Basted seams can be undone or removed without too much effort.

BIAS refers to the line obtained by folding a piece of fabric on the diagonal. A fabric that is cut on the bias will stretch under its own weight. It is necessary to let pieces of fabric that are cut on the bias hang from a hanger for a few days before continuing onto assembly.

BINDING TAPE is a lightweight tape, usually made of cotton or synthetic fiber, that is available in a wide range of colors. It is used to strengthen garment hems and belts.

A **BUTTON FLAP** is a doubled strip of fabric onto which the button loops or buttonholes are embroidered.

A **BUTTONHOLE** is an opening edged by embroidered stitching and whose purpose is to allow a button to pass through.

A **BUTTON LOOP** is a buttonhole that is made by taking a small strip of fabric, a chain of thread (round or embroidered button loop) or even a piece of bias binding and attaching it to the edge of a tab (mitered button loop).

A **CASING** is a hem finishing that is open at both ends and into which a cord may be inserted. This feature makes it possible for you to tighten part of an item around the waistline, the neck, or the wrist. Casings can also be used to create adjustable openings on some decorative items.

CLIPPING means to create cuts along rounded seams to give them greater ease.

A **DART** is a fold, triangular in shape, that is sewn onto the wrong side of a piece of fabric and whose purpose is to limit the shape of an item while providing fullness.

DRAPE corresponds to the vertical fall of a garment or of a decorative item.

EASE is the fullness that you give to a garment; it gives a garment additional room.

EASING involves carefully stretching out the weft of a fabric using a steam iron.

EDGING is a finishing technique that involves applying a piece of bias binding, piping, or braiding to the edge of a completed item.

FACING is fabric used to line the wrong side of a collar or a button flap. In general, it is made from the same fabric as that of the main item itself.

FLAG MARKS are the red threads or the narrow strips of paper attached to the edge of fabric selvages to indicate the presence of fabric imperfections.

A **FLAP** is a strip of fabric that is used to cover the opening of a bag (see page 150) or of a pocket on a jacket or a pair of pants (flapped pocket). It may be sewn on separately or be completed as part of the item itself.

GATHERING refers to the formation of small regular or irregular folds by running one or two threads into a piece of fabric and pulling on them in opposite directions.

HALF-WIDTH FOLDED fabric has been folded in half, right sides together, and rolled onto a rectangular board. This kind of folding is also known as a lengthwise fold.

A **HEM** is a finishing formed by a fold, single or double, along the edge of an assembled item to conceal the raw edges. It may be with or without an allowance.

A **HEM FOLD** is a folding in of the edge of an item onto the wrong side of the fabric and is used when completing a hem or applying a lining.

INTERFACING refers to the process of giving rigidity to a piece by lining it with a stiff fabric or by applying a piece of fusible fabric onto its wrong side using an iron.

LOOPS are rings of fabric sewn onto a garment to hold a belt in place.

A MITER is made by folding the excess fabric at a corner or on a hem bordering a corner into a right angle.

OVERALL WIDTH refers to the width of a piece of fabric, including the selvages.

OVERCASTING refers to the application of an overcast stitch to the edges of a piece of fabric, either by hand or by machine, to help forestall fraying.

A PRESSING CLOTH should be made from 100% white cotton that does not pill and should be washed before use so as to remove any layers of finish. It is used during assembly to press seams open and to flatten darts and helps keep the iron from lustering or burning the fabric. It should be moistened rather than soaked. The steam iron has not yet managed to eliminate the need for a pressing cloth.

PUCKERING is the unfortunate result of a seam whose stitches are too tight and which end up gathering or creasing the surface of the fabric. When that happens, undo the seam, adjust the settings on your sewing machine, and start the stitching over again.

A RAGLAN SEAM is a diagonal seam that is used to join a sleeve to an armhole.

A RIDGE is the crest formed by an edge-to-edge seam; it should not warp or buckle.

ROUNDING means smoothly fitting around the intended curvature of a rounded part by clipping the seam allowance or attaching a bias piece to stretch around it.

ROUNDING OUT refers to the act of altering the hem on a skirt or a dress. The dimensions of the hem should be determined with respect to the distance from the ground to the hem rather than from the waistline to the hem. There is a small instrument with a sliding foot and fitted with a piece of tailor's chalk that makes it possible to trace the hem directly onto the item that is being modeled.

A SELVAGE is made from the warp threads that are situated at each end of the crosswise span of a piece of fabric.

The SEWING MACHINE PEDAL is a rheostat. On some sewing machines, the stitch speed is set using this pedal.

The SLEEVE BOARD is a small narrow board consisting of a foot and a padded, coated surface. It is used for pressing sleeves or the legs of pants.

The STRAIGHT GRAIN or lengthwise grain, which is indicated by double-headed arrows on pattern pieces, is parallel to the selvages of the fabric; it is the direction in which the warp threads run.

SURPLUS refers to the excess fullness that is found on the inner folds of a hem or in a rounded seam.

TOPSTITCHING involves using a straight stitch on the right side of an item to shadow an existing seam at a distance of a few eighths of an inch.

The WARP of woven fabrics refers to the threads that run parallel to the selvages. These threads do not stretch; theirs is the direction chosen for the lengthwise orientation of sewn items.

A woven fabric that is WARPED is one where the weft threads were deformed during weaving so that they are no longer perpendicular to the selvages. You will have to correct the orientation of the weft by stretching or by pressing the fabric with the aid of a pressing cloth, then setting the corners using a plastic triangle.

The WEFT refers to, for woven fabrics, the threads that run perpendicular to the selvages. The weft threads of a piece of fabric are more stretchable than the warp threads; they may be stretched to some degree.

A YOKE is a sewn or decorated piece of fabric onto which other pieces are sewn; it serves as a means of keeping them all together.

A ZIGZAG STITCH is a stitch that is made on a sewing machine. Among its many usages, the zigzag stitch may be used to overcast the edges of fabrics (see the zigzag stitch on page 25).

Detailed of Contents

INDEX

Metric Conversion Chart
MM=Millemeters CM=Centimeters

Inches	MM	CM		Inches	CM
⅛	3	0.3		4	10.2
¼	6	0.6		4½	11.4
⅜	10	1.0		5	12.7
½	13	1.3		6	15.2
⅝	16	1.6		7	17.8
¾	19	1.9		8	20.3
⅞	22	2.2		9	22.9
1	25	2.5		10	25.4
1¼	32	3.2		11	27.9
1½	38	3.8		12	30.5
1¾	44	4.4		13	33.0
2	51	5.1		14	35.6
2½	64	6.4		15	38.1
3	76	7.6		16	40.6
3½	89	8.9			